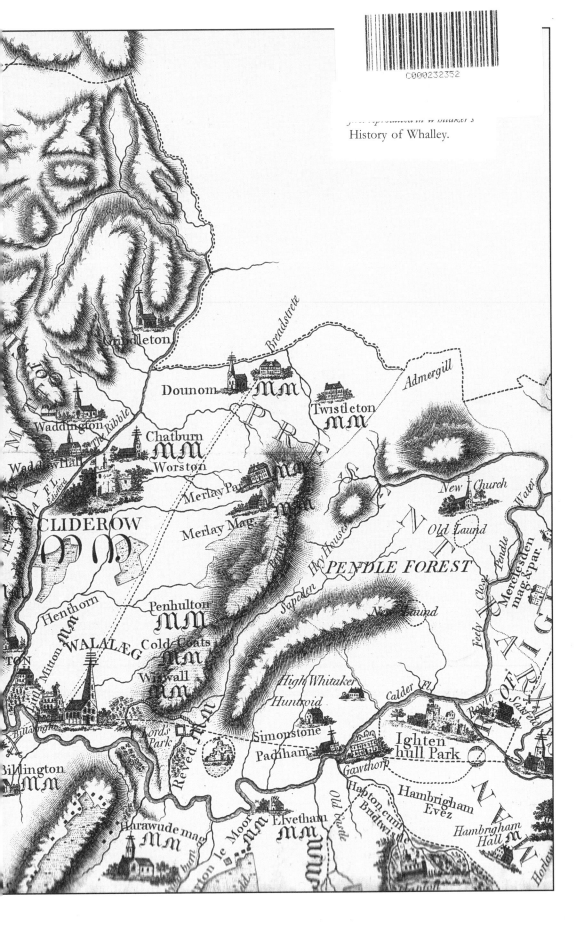

History of Whalley.

BOWLAND AND PENDLE HILL

BOWLAND AND PENDLE HILL

W. R. MITCHELL

Phillimore

2004

Published by
PHILLIMORE & CO. LTD
Shopwyke Manor Barn, Chichester, West Sussex, England

ISBN 1 86077 285 4

Printed and bound in Great Britain by
MPG BOOKS LTD
Bodmin, Cornwall

CONTENTS

LIST OF ILLUSTRATIONS

Frontispiece: Dunsop Head

ACKNOWLEDGEMENTS

Dr Thomas Dunham Whitaker's tomes on Whalley and Craven, published in 1801 and 1805 respectively, were essential reading. His study of the Archdeaconry of Craven included Great Bowland, which until recently was part of Yorkshire. The copy of *History of Craven* I borrowed from a friend had been purchased at a reduced price. The vendor said the book's condition was poor and someone had 'scribbled' on nearly every page. The scribbles turned out to be valuable annotations, in copperplate.

Colonel J. Parker, of Browsholme, a notable local historian, fired my interest in Bowland by relating stories of his forebears and giving me a copy of the paper he read to the Society of Genealogists in 1926. Robert R. Parker, who presides over the estate today, allowed me to copy some family pictures. From Lord Clitheroe, of Downham Hall, I heard of the life and times of the Asshetons, who had moved to Downham in the year Elizabeth I was crowned. The late Major J. E. E. Yorke, of Halton Place, was the proverbial fount of knowledge, recalling other local landowners and days when he rode in Gisburne Park with Lord Ribblesdale, the last of his line. J. Weld Blundell, of Leagram Park, told me about the local strain of white cattle.

The staff of the Pendle Heritage Centre, Barrowford, was most co-operative. At the Reference Library at Clitheroe – a treasure house for the local historian – I was directed to appropriate files of written and photographic material. Members of the Chipping Local History Society produced some choice items from their library in St Mary's Old School. For information about Stonyhurst College and the Tolkien Trail I am indebted to Jonathan Hewat, Admissions and Marketing Manager. The College has a fine museum, the curator of which is Mrs Jan Graffius.

Mary Dawber loaned me prints of old-time Clitheroe. Phil Hudson, of Hudson History, Settle, copied old engravings. Having tape-recorded interviews with Bowlanders over many years, I was able to listen again to tales related by George Robinson of Slaidburn, Vic Robinson of Bolton-by-Bowland, Doris Wells of Rimington and Tom Cowking of Rathmell. Jack Cottam, son of Harry Cottam, resident engineer for Stocks Reservoir, in the upper Hodder, described the transformation of a once-quiet farming valley into a major water undertaking. I turned up notes made during meetings with Jessica Lofthouse, a prolific writer on Lancashire and the Dale Country. She had been associated 'on mother's side', with the Reads, who sprang from a community of that name and 'worked their way round Pendle Hill to settle at Clitheroe in the 16th century'.

Ready help came from Susan Bourne, Curator of Towneley Hall Art Gallery & Museum, from Diana Rushton, Community History Manager at the Central Library in Blackburn, and from Vivien Meath, editor of the *Clitheroe Advertiser & Times*. Peter F. Parkes, of Castle Cement, sent me information about a notable local industry. Donald McKay, Principal Planning Officer, provided an update of the Forest of Bowland relating to its status as an Area of Outstanding Natural Beauty.

Uncredited illustrations are from my own collection. The map in line of the Forest of Bowland on page two was penned by Christine Denmead. I acknowledge with thanks the origin of the following pictures: Blackburn Public Library 62; Edmundson Buck 105, 109, 142; Browsholme Hall, courtesy of Robert Parker 37, 38, 40, 41, 42, 114; Mary Dawber 98, 120, 121; Peter Delap 34, 116; Clitheroe Reference Library 63, 90, 91, 92, 122, 128, 129; Lord Clitheroe 58, 59; Peter Fox 100, 101; Charles Haworth, from *A History of Blackburn Waterworks* made available by the local library 6, 7, 12, 30, 31, 32, 148, 149; Frank Hird's *Lancashire Stories* 47; Knowsley Council of Voluntary Service 86, 87, 88; Pendle Heritage Centre 46, 51, 52, 53, 54, 123, 127, 136, 146; Misses Pickles 143; Stonyhurst College 79; The National Gallery 71; *The Preston Guardian* 133, 134; Reads of Clitheroe, 118; George Walker's *The Costume of Yorkshire* 83, 84, 85, 125, 126, 130; Dr T.D. Whitaker's histories of Whalley and Craven 3, 9, 13, 14, 18, 21, 22, 84, 85, 117, 150.

For
John Miller
Pendle Heritage Centre

An Overview

The medieval Forest of Bowland was unlike a forest in the modern sense of massed trees. It comprised a tract of outlying, partly-wooded land and was a hunting preserve for a Norman king or his nominees. Today the name Forest of Bowland applies to an Area of Outstanding Natural Beauty that extends from the plains of the Fylde to the valleys of Ribble and Wenning, with Pendle Hill forming a notable separate feature. The AONB has, indeed, absorbed several old-time forests. A London journalist described Bowland as 'a sunken, secret corner of Lancashire', yet for centuries, until local government reorganisation in 1974, it was mainly in Yorkshire, which extended to within sight of the Irish Sea and gave Lancashire a waist like a wasp. Bowland tenants were exonerated from jury service in York because of the travel difficulties. There was delight in Bowland when the Ordnance Survey, using a computerised technique, established that a barn near Dunsop Bridge was the precise centre of the British Isles.

Bowland's cluster of whaleback hills rises from low-lying peripheral areas. Pendle Hill is grandly isolated, with a shape that suggested to one visitor an upside-down boat or a ridge-tent with one end slightly shorter than the other. Viewed on a map, the 300-square mile Area of Outstanding Natural Beauty has a neat appearance. Dunsop Bridge, which is at the heart of Bowland, stands where several watercourses meet and mingle with the river Hodder, 'pleasant stream' of the Celtic folk, which is the main watercourse. It merges with the Ribble at Hodder Foot, near Mitton, where ledges of rock end in sheer drops into chilly depths. A.T.R. Houghton, late Clerk to the Ribble Board of Conservators, wrote in 1952, 'More than one keen angler, striving to cover the pool, has stepped forward on to nothing but water and found himself swimming for his life.' You cannot go far in Bowland without hearing the tinkle of water in a brook feeding the Lune, Ribble or Wyre.

Wards Stone (no apostrophe), the highest point in the Forest of Bowland, has a retinue of fells that are only marginally lower. Second in the list of highest fells is aptly named White Hill, its summit being composed of coarse grasses rather than heather. A Victorian visitor, J.G. Shaw, wrote, 'One may tramp for miles on these uplands without apparently getting much nearer the top.' Three roads give through-passage in this northern area. The best-known route runs

I

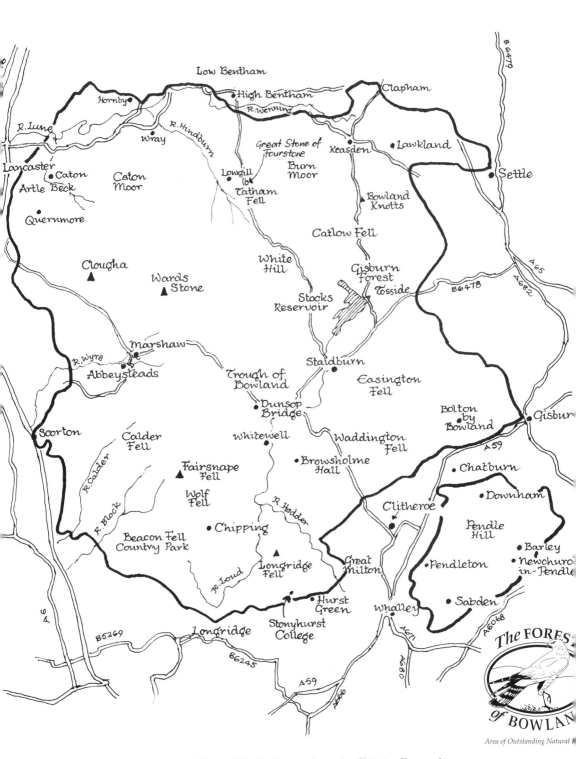

Forest of Bowland map, drawn by Christine Denmead.

through the Trough, the environ of which is a delight to motorists in late summer. Then flowering ling seems to tint the underbellies of passing clouds. In winter, red grouse, normally shy and wild, peck delicately at heather within a few feet of passing vehicles.

Historians in Bowland still quibble over the name. Signposts erected by the old Bowland Rural District Council in the 1930s featured the silhouette of a chubby little bowman, with taut bowstring. It seemed appropriate to an area called Bowland, but imbues it with a romantic connotation it probably does not deserve. Tom Smith, the Victorian historian of Chipping, had no doubt about the origin. Bowland derived its name from having been famous in Saxon times for the exercise of archery. Opinions are varied. Colonel Parker, of Browsholme Hall, after noting that the older inhabitants

2 *Forest signs near Roughlee.*

referred to Bolland, added, 'Outsiders call and spell it Bowland from a silly notion (encouraged by Dr Whitaker) that it was a land of Bows and Arrows.'

Boeland, the earliest traceable spelling, became Boweland in the 13th century. It may refer to a river feature or to pastoral farming. A popular notion, shared by Colonel Parker, is that it is derived from the Celtic *booa* and Old Norse *bol*, alluding to cattle. In 1066, when the Normans moved in, the upland valleys of Bowland were already the setting for cattle-farms. Their products included oxen to be used as draft animals and also dairy products – cheese and butter. The Normans allowed such a cattle-ranch to continue, with the Norman-French name of *vaccary*, from *vache*, meaning a cow. Sheep were first mentioned on the southern fells in the 16th century. Cunliffe Shaw, historian of Lancashire forests, mentioned the presence of 'ancient stints for cattle and sheep' at Totridge and Fence Brow in 1571. Yet in monastic times pasturage on the adjacent limestone district of Craven was the setting for huge sheep farms. Wool from the great Cistercian abbeys of Yorkshire was exported in large quantities to the Continent.

In the Forest of Pendle the wooden huts used by cow-keepers were known as *booths*, from a Norse word for a farmhouse. The word *booth* was to survive in the names of some of the permanent settlements. After about three centuries, the *vaccaries* changed their form and some of the cow-keepers became yeoman farmers.

3   *Thomas Dunham Whitaker, historian.*

4   *Dunsop Bridge, the central village.*

The spirit of that time lingered on. A modern writer, Ella Pontefract, was able to write of Bowland, 'Here is yeoman England, dreaming of the past'. She described Bowland as 'a soft, sylvan country that breaks suddenly and unexpectedly into heathy common, moor and fell.' J. S. Fletcher, in 1901, felt isolated and commented on the virtual absence of tourists. 'Bowland lies far out of the track of the railway-engine and has no high road transecting it.'

From the high moors one might view the Lakeland Fells, the Three Peaks of Yorkshire or Pendle Hill. Travellers on the Trough route who break their journey at the Jubilee Tower have a fine-weather view of what in the distance is the pencil-thin form of Blackpool Tower. The owner of nearby Hare Appletree built the Bowland tower to mark the 1887 Jubilee of Queen Victoria. The name Ribble, for the river that sweeps down the valley separating Bowland and Pendle, probably relates to its status as a boundary. The border that lay between Northumbria and Mercia is a possibility. Early weather forecasters on the 'wireless' distinguished between weather 'north of the Ribble' and that to the south. Clitheroe folk referred to a shower from the north as a 'Chipping Duster'.

As the town of Clitheroe waxed, the Norman castle waned. Clitheroe became the second oldest borough in Lancashire (the oldest, for the record, is Wigan). The castle was slighted at the time of the Civil War, though a hoary tale relates that a hole in the east wall of the keep was caused when the devil threw a rock from Pendle Hill. In an early drawing of the castle, an artist added a few windows for effect. Clitheroe became partly industrialised but never lost its market town appeal nor, because of the intervening Pendle Hill, did it become part of the East Lancashire conurbation.

In dull weather, one might reflect on Dr Whitaker's comments on the climate. To him, Bowland presented 'the broad and bulky masses of its hills to those copious exhalations, which, rising in the Irish Sea, or even in the Atlantic, are driven by the continual prevalence of westerly winds against their sides'. Its summers were often ungenial, its autumns lost in fogs, its grain damp and musty, its fruits crude and unmellowed. The situation was somewhat better than in primeval times, when the vales steamed with unwholesome swamps.

On the old Yorkshire-Lancashire divide, map-names aptly describe the topography. The old county boundary was marked on the map at intervals by the words 'pile of stones', an ancient form of waymarking. The *beck* of the Pennine Dales has become a *brook*. The Pennine *gill*, for a water-carved, wooded valley, is rendered *clough* (and pronounced 'cloo'). Evocative names include Fiendsdale Head, Strandsdale Brook, Kite Clough and Black Clough Head. Beyond the heads of Whitendale and Brennand is another little-known region of *crags, mosses, sykes, intakes* and, of course, yet more *cloughs*, the tributaries of Whitendale draining Stony Clough, Costy Clough and Little Costy Clough. In the Brennand valley are Folds Clough, Well Spring Clough and Far Pasture Clough.

Those who follow the road from Slaidburn to High Bentham experience a sense of remoteness in uplands inhabited by sheep and grouse. Across the upper valley of the Hodder is Catlow, one of the big sheep farms. Visitors resting their elbows on a parapet of the Cross o'Greet bridge view the infant river and also a bold horizontal mark on the fellside made when a railtrack was laid to convey stone from Jumbles Quarry, now clogged with bracken. The road east of Stocks Reservoir crests at Bowland Knotts, an area of weathered gritstone. Walkers using the track over Salter Fell, also known as Hornby Road, are on the line of a Roman road linking Ribchester with Burrow in the valley of the Lune. The rivers Hindburn, Roeburn and Wenning drain this northern side of Bowland, with Hindburn joining the Roeburn at Wray. Hornby Castle, best viewed from a bank of the Wenning near the road bridge, was a Royalist garrison in the Civil War and was subsequently a gentleman's house.

5 *Boundary Stone, Trough of Bowland.*

6   *Lower Hodder Bridge, drawn by Charles Haworth.*

Bowland's extensive grouse moors were long regarded as forbidden territory for walkers. In 1996, agreement between various landowners and the County Council provided increased access. The water authority has a tolerant attitude towards responsible walkers. The special Access Areas are on Clougha, Tarnbrook, Fairsnape, Wolf and Saddle Fells. A walker trudging along an official path from Tower Lodge to Wards Stone, the highest point in Bowland, 1,836ft/560m., passes close to where the moorland reverberates to the calls of a vast gullery. There are two summits, east and west, the last-named being marked by the huge boulder after which the hill was named. Some of Bowland's special features are revealed in a walk from Dunsop Bridge towards the head of Whitendale, 'valley of the white ling'. The river sparkles between belts of trees adorning the lower slopes of domed hills that are thatched with heather. At the end of June moist areas on the hills are adorned by the so-called cotton-grass, which is actually a sedge. A mass of fluffy white seed-heads give the impression of a summer fall of snow.

7   *Brennand Valley, drawn by Charles Haworth.*

Cattle in small groups graze the grassy slopes. Good weather is indicated if they are on the skyline, with light showing between their bodies and the ground. Nicholas Assheton, visiting the valley in 1617, found the area 'overrun with good deare'. He slew a

8   *Clitheroe in the 1960s.*

knobber (a stag with its first antlers) and a calf. In the valley of the Wyre, which lies to the west, the scenic variety includes adjacent 'black' ground (heather) and 'white' land (grasses). Eastwards, in Bowland, the landscape takes the form of ridges. The name Salter Fell, for high ground between Lune and Upper Hodder, evokes a time when Gals (ponies) bore salt from the coastal regions to the farms and villages of the hinterland. Large quantities of salt were used to preserve meat being stored for winter use. Alfred Wainwright, who compiled hand-written and hand-illustrated guides to Lakeland and the Pennines, considered the Salter Fell route to be 'possibly the finest moorland walk in England'.

Davis and Lee, writing about Bowland in 1878, mentioned strong ploughlands, rich pastures, plus 'wide expanses of unenclosed moor which cannot be altered in spirit since the days when the area was the hunting ground of the de Lacys'. Cyril Harrington, in *The Dalesman* magazine, asserted that the feudal organisation of the land and many of the old usages continued unaltered until modern times. 'As a result, the Middle Ages seem closer to us here than elsewhere.' The eldest son of a landowner served in the Gulf War. A member of the family had fought overseas – at Agincourt.

The Forest of Bowland's status as Crown land ended when, following the Restoration, Charles II gave it to General Monk, who was elevated to Duke of Albemarle. Yet a royal flavour endured. The Duchy of Lancaster, which owns 5,500 acres/2,227ha. of Bowland along the Hodder Valley, traces its beginnings to Edmund, son of Henry III, who was given the 'county, honour and castle' of Lancaster and the title Earl of Lancaster. His grandson, Henry, was created Duke of Lancaster in 1351. As a consequence of special ducal rights, the County of Lancaster became a 'County Palatine'. The monarch is toasted in Lancashire as 'The Queen, Duke of Lancaster'. Royal visits are not unusual. George V, visiting Abbeystead for a shoot in 1926, stayed for a week and attended church on the Sunday morning. Following the death of Lady Sefton in 1980, the Duke of Westminster purchased the Abbeystead estate and his guests have included members of the royal family. George VI purchased for the Duchy of Lancaster the old Towneley estate at Whitewell. The present Queen finds special enjoyment in visiting the area.

9 *Stonyhurst, as portrayed in Whitaker's* History of Whalley.

10 *Hornby Castle and the Wenning, Lunesdale.*

Bowland has a rich and varied folklore. Old crones living on the southern flanks of Pendle Hill were mistaken for witches. So vivid are the stories told of the Pendle witches that at Hallowe'en the superstitious expected to see them cavorting in the air on broomsticks. Moorland sprites abounded. The Ordnance Survey map including the intersection of the parishes of Pendleton, Sabden and Whalley shows a feature known as Jeppe Knave Grave. Jeppe was supposed to be a medieval character who was so wicked that no one wanted him to be buried locally. Each parish agreed to take one-third of him. In truth, Jeppe's grave is a plundered Bronze-Age cairn. A 17th-century record of a boundary dispute mentions 'a Ston for rubinge of cattle'. What happened to this standing stone?

At Slaidburn, an inn was named *Hark to Bounty* after a hound with an especially melodious voice. The *Sun Inn* at Chipping is haunted by the ghost of Lizzy Dean, a servant girl who, in 1835, was engaged to a man who married another woman. Lizzy, aged 20, hanged herself in the attic of the inn. Her last request was that she might be buried under the path of the church, so that her former lover would have to walk over her when attending Sunday services. Bowland and Pendle churchyards are full of surprises. At St Mary's, Newchurch-in-Pendle, is a granite memorial to James Aitken of Dundee, who was among those following Bonnie Prince Charlie on his march from Scotland in 1745. James died at Newchurch in 1794. In the same churchyard is a memorial plaque to the memory of a former vicar, the Rev. J. S. Barnes Wallis, and his wife Margaret. He was the nephew of Dr Barnes Wallis, the inventor of the Bouncing Bomb used in the Dam Busters' raid during the Second World War.

11   *Pendle Heritage Centre, Barrowford.*

The local government reorganisation of 1974, in which Yorkshire's historic major share of Bowland was transferred to Lancashire, brought to an end a curious state that had existed at Whitewell, near the heart of the district. It had been described as 'a peculiar village, consisting of an inn, a church and a school. The population consists of the inn-keeper and his family, for even the Vicar lives a mile or two away. The flock of the latter is scattered like the sheep all over the hills. At best there is a sparse congregation and the schoolchildren have to trudge miles and miles to their lessons or come by the carrier's cart.' Consider the situation in detail. St Michael's, at Whitewell, was a chapelry in the ancient parish of Whalley until 1878, when it received parish status. The ecclesiastical parish of 15 ½ square miles was divided between the West Riding and the County Palatine of Lancashire. Educational matters were dealt with at Wakefield, county town of the West Riding, and health matters were dealt with at Settle. Whitewell parish lay in Ewecross for registration purposes and yet was situated in the rural district of Bowland. Two curiously detached pieces of land were Countess Adelaide's Flatts – meadowland by the river at the edge of Slaidburn – and Harrop, in its secluded little valley in the same area. Whitewell had no village as such. The church was close to the river Hodder, yet the vicarage stood three miles away and at an elevation of 650ft. Whitewell's population of 500 consisted mainly of tenant farmers and their families.

Such local quirks and fancies contribute to the special appeal of Bowland. Local life and traditions are sustained, though tourism now vies with farming as a means of making a living. Historic hotels and inns maintain the spirit of good hospitality. Socially, there is a decline in native folk and a rise in the number of off-comers, as they used to be known. Old farmsteads have been adapted and modernised as dwellings, and redundant barns converted into homes or country retreats, inflating prices for property. Newcomers are quickly absorbed and the spirit of the past survives in wideflung moors, quiet dales, old estates, unspoilt villages and venerable farmsteads.

One

LANDFORM, VEGETATION
AND WILDLIFE

Geology

In the north of Bowland, the visual element is a block of gritstone moors extending
from about 183m. to 550m. above sea level. The celebrated Trough of Bowland,
on the main road through the district, is geologically no more than a steep-sided
river valley formed by a small tributary of the Hodder that wore down the
gritstone. The southern part of the area is distinctive in that the fells are more
detached. Pendle Hill, a major feature, stands in grand isolation.

G. Bernard Wood, a Yorkshire writer and photographer, described Bowland
as 'another limestone area, but in a minor key'. Its villages did not have to
contend with towering scars and incipient potholes. 'Here, the limestone wears
a gentler garb.' The Ribble Valley is classed geologically as a rejuvenated
Carboniferous landscape, which means that over millions of years the overlying
rocks laid down since those times have been eroded away. Carboniferous limestone
now lies close to the surface. It gives the landscape its bright and cheerful
appearance.

The Clitheroe Anticline extends from Waddington Fell to Pendle Hill.
Limestone has been bared in the form of a line of conical limebanks, composed
of a creamy-grey rock. They are commonly known as reef knolls, the thickest
being up to 305m. At the core of the anticline, where the village of Chatburn
stands, the limestone has a thickness of over 360m. When excavations took place
near Chatburn for the Clitheroe-Whalley by-pass the workmen removed 18m. of
limestone.

An old couplet declares, 'Worsaw, Warren, Ridge and Crow; Four limestone
knolls all in a row.' The Clitheroe district, renowned for 'lime, latin and law', is
famous in the scientific community for its variety of fossils. These are most
conspicuous in the reef knolls, which grew in the warmer and shallower water.
Salthill Quarry, where a geological trail has been set out, in part covered a reef
knoll. It offers visitors the humbling experience of seeing exposures of limestone
with fossils from Lower Carboniferous times.

A guide to Salthill describes the conditions in which many primitive forms
of life throve as 'an environment of warm shallow water and gentle currents'.
Limestone was laid down as calcium carbonate, from the skeletal remains of

12   White cow in the park at Gisburn, drawn by Charles Haworth.

incalculable numbers of marine creatures living in an area somewhat south of the equator. The process took place over a period lasting from about 350 to 190 million years ago. When the weather was semi-tropical, coral reefs were formed. Here were to be found the richest forms of life that would become fossils. In the main deposit, most life-forms were minute, to be studied through a microscope. Among the larger fossils are the remains of crinoids, also known as sea-lilies, and gastropods, which resembled large snails.

The remains of this distant world, accumulating on the bed of the sea, were compressed into limestone. The theory of Continental Drift accounts for their present position in the northern hemisphere. Muddy water, caused by material from a land-mass to the north, led to the formation of a 'blue' type of limestone. In Bowland, the folding of the strata, as in the valleys of Sykes, Brennand and Whitendale, has exposed limestone inliers through which, as through a window, it is possible to see the older rocks below.

Clitheroe evolved on an elongated limestone knoll, with a castle at one end and the parish church at the other, these features being linked by the shops and inns of the main street. In early times, sacks of lime were distributed on the backs of packhorses. It was estimated that between 500 and 1,000 loads passed through the town in a single day. Gals (packhorses) bore loads of lime to Burnley and returned with loads of coal. Disused kilns are a reminder of the days when lime was burnt for domestic use and also to sweeten acid land.

Resuming the geological story, the seas retreated and the land was covered by dense tropical forest. In this period the Coal Measures were laid down. Deltaic conditions and luxuriant plant growth were responsible for the Bowland Shales – black shales, banded occasionally by limestone and sandstone. Some of the black shales are highly organic, containing a large proportion of petroleum, as well as small amounts of uranium. Fossil goniatites are located in the shales exposed by cloughs on the northern flank of Pendle Hill. Vast quantities of sand swept down by a huge northern river formed the gritstone that gives Pendle and some Bowland hills impervious caps, protecting from weathering the underlying softer rocks.

During the million-year spectacular known as the Ice Age, glacial ice that advanced from Lakeland into Craven split up like fingers of a hand. One finger gouged out the valley of the Hodder, coating the lower slopes with a mush we call boulder-clay. At lower levels the soils that have a high clay content are said to be *gleyed*. The present shape of the Ribble Valley results from the most recent period of glaciation that ended a mere 10,000 years ago. A heady rush of melt-water down the Hodder created the gorge near Whitewell.

Vegetation

When the Pleistocene ice cleared, tundral conditions prevailed for a long period. The first trees were birch and willow. With a change of climate, other species of tree spread across the face of the landscape. Thick beds of peat testify to a high rainfall, to poor drainage and low temperatures in which moorland vegetation is slow to decompose. Within historical times most of the Bowland area was well-timbered, with trees growing up to 500m. as dictated by the underlying rock and condition of the soil. At the time of human intervention Bowland was undoubtedly well-wooded – a natural forest indeed. Sessile oak throve in suitable gritstone locations up to an elevation of about 500m. or to within a few hundred feet of the highest point. Ash, elm and hazel flourished in the limestone areas. On stiff and clayey soils hornbeam grew to an impressive size. Alder flourished in wet areas, such as riversides.

'Relict' areas of the former woodland cover exist in some of the dry cloughs, where there has been difficulty of access and farm management has been slight or non-existent. The species growing here include sessile oak, downy birch, rowan and perhaps holly. In moist cloughs the ash may be dominant, with hazel and bird cherry. The thorn, also known as quickthorn, was a favourite hedgerow tree. Blackthorn is relatively common, the sloes (fruit) being the basis of sloe-gin. Private landowners beautified the environs of their halls with ornamental species. Eighteenth-century fashion encompassed new woodland composed of beech and ash. Later, stands of Scots pine were popular. Rhododendrons, which provided cover for game, became leggy and almost impossible to eradicate. Water authorities, as in the Black Moss area south of Pendle, planted a considerable number of beech and sycamore.

Since the Second World War large tracts of Bowland have become coniferous forest, the species including those from the New World such as sitka spruce and lodge-pole pine. Larch and Norway spruce are popular in Bowland. Sitka spruce is a favourite because it has especially quick growth and yields good timber. David Douglas, the Scottish botanist who found it growing on the coastal strip of British Columbia in Canada, introduced the species to Britain in 1831. The Bowland 'tops' are boggy and acidic. Here is found a mosaic of plant species – heather, bilberry, cowberry and crowberry. Purple moor-grass forms tussocks in areas of poor management but generally the Bowland moors are well maintained. By many stretches of rivers grows a lusty newcomer, the Himalayan balsam, which flicks its seeds away using a natural spring device.

Wildlife

Brown bears and beavers roamed free until about 1000 AD. The ancient fauna of Bowland included the wild boar. Accounts associated with the Forest of Pendle for 1295-6 reveal that 80 wild boar were sold for £3 6s. 1d. (A modern attraction for visitors is a wild boar park near Chipping.) Baked wild boar graced the table when Sir Richard Hoghton entertained King James I at Hoghton Tower. The wolf's association with Bowland lasted until the 14th century. Camden, writing in 1600, recalled the species in relation to the type of Lancashire cattle of olden days, which were 'long-horned with thick hides and shaggy hair, hardy and active, capable of thriving through severe winters on the upland pastures and withstanding the attack of wolves'.

Tosside, the hill-top village between Hodder and Ribble, is said to have been named after the fox, but did a she-wolf suckle her young at Whelpstone Crag, a remote and high rocky place on a long ridge extending from Tosside? 'Woofus', the local name for Wolf Fell, above Chipping, probably meant wolves' house (lair). Wolf House Pike, on Parlick Pike, also near Chipping, was the site of a small refuge for people 'when pressed by hungry and ferocious wolves'. It also served as a look-out. 'Farmers could be warned of the approach of wolves, which in wintertime, especially, became bold.' Many tales about wolves should be taken with the proverbial pinch of salt. They rarely if ever attacked humans. (The

13   *White bull, as portrayed in Whitaker's* History of Craven.

ancient wolf-house became the nucleus of a residence of a branch of the Sherburne family.)

White cattle may have descended from wild stock. Yet within historical times they were emparked, some of them at Hoghton Tower, near Preston; a horned white bull figured on the crest of the de Hoghton family whose 'supporters' were two white bulls. Kenneth Whitehead, in his study of the Ancient Wild Cattle of England, wondered whether the cattle in the park were horned or polled like those at nearby Gisburne Park. The Gisburne stock, which belonged to the Listers, later Lords Ribblesdale, was received from Whalley Abbey at the time of the Dissolution. The engraver Bewick recorded they were 'lured by music', which might have been a romantic addition to an old story. A white bull was an impressive beast, weighing

14   *Skull of a species of sheep formerly kept at Gisburn, from Whitaker's* History of Craven.

almost a ton. The *White Bull* inn in the village commemorates this association. It was at Hoghton Tower, in Lancashire, that James I knighted a prime cut which became 'sirloin'. A herd of white cattle is kept at Leagram Hall; at the time of writing there are 13 breeding animals out of a total number of twenty-five.

Red deer moved into the north country in the wake of receding ice. In a well-wooded setting like Bowland they would have the food and shelter that enabled them to fulfil their potential, unlike their cousins in bleaker lands further north which would be appreciably smaller. The roe deer was another native species. The Normans introduced the fallow deer, a species with distinctive spade-like antlers. The last of the cosseted deer was slaughtered about 1805. Almost a century later Peter Ormerod of Wyresdale and Lord Ribblesdale of Gisburn, needing sporty deer for the Ribblesdale Buckhounds to pursue, introduced a few dark-phase fallow. When these were hunted out they brought in a stock of sika, an Asiatic species, obtaining them from the deer park at Powerscourt, south of Dublin.

The sika deer were emparked near Gisburn. Selected animals were carted to the hunting ground and released. It was hoped to round them up in the evening and return them to the park but inevitably some escaped. Landowners were concerned at the damage they caused to trees. Peter Ormerod would occasionally

15   *Young curlew in a Bowland meadow.*

16   *Sika stag. The species was introduced to Bowland early in the 20th century.*

arrive at the home of an aggrieved squire with a bundle of young trees as compensation. One man, noting a pathetically small number of saplings, retorted, 'Some people can be bribed and I'm one of them – but not with tuppence.' In recent years, roe deer have returned to wooded areas. Two mammalian introductions from the New World are the grey squirrel and mink, the last-named having built up its numbers from escapees from Lancashire fur farms.

The image of a hen harrier – slim, long-tailed – is the logo of the Forest of Bowland. In the 1960s birdwatchers had to be content with a glimpse of a wintering harrier in the vicinity of Stocks Reservoir. The species is now well established on the Bowland moors, where it may be seen in low-gliding flight, the long narrow wings being held in a shallow V-shape. Much more typical of Bowland is the red grouse, a localised form of the willow grouse of far northern lands, which thrives on well-tended and keepered moors where heather is 'swiddened' (periodically burnt in strips) to provide growth at various stages. Another requirement is that predators like foxes and crows should be kept down. A dependence on heather for food means that the grouse is a virtual prisoner on the moors. It is joined in spring by wading birds such as the golden plover, its dark mantle flecked with gold. The rare dotterel, on passage migration, is seen on Pendle Hill in May. The pheasant, reared extensively for sport, is a descendant of ancient jungle fowl. Canada geese, now numerous at Stocks Reservoir and also on the lakes at Stonyhurst, is a New World species that has been in this country for several centuries.

Charles Waterton (1782-1865), naturalist and pioneer conservationist, was educated at Stonyhurst. The college inherited a collection of stuffed birds and beasts collected mainly in South America. He did not 'stuff' in the conventional way any creature he wished to preserve; his procedure involved stiffening the skin and preserving the plumage without recourse to such aids as wire.

Two

THE HUMAN ELEMENT

Early Settlement

Whitaker, in his *History of Whalley*, published in 1801, surveyed what he described as a bleak and barren district. He investigated the progress of the Roman conquests. He saw the Angles as 'a rude and unlettered tribe from the forest of Germany introducing their laws and language (the basis of our own)'. Whitaker considered the effects of the Norman Conquest on the state of property. There had been a gradual surrender of primitive manors to the superior lord and 'the successive grants of the same to a new race of feudal chiefs, the ancestors of many ancient families yet subsisting'.

Evidence of prehistoric activity remains sparse. Crude pottery, probably of Neolithic age (*c.*4500 BC), has been found near what is now the village of Slaidburn. Neolithic folk who lived round Pendle made polished stone axes. An improvement in the climate during the Bronze Age (*c.*2500 BC) led to a spread of families from the free-draining limestone country on to the gritstone. It was also a period when there was trade with Ireland. Along the trade routes passed coveted items such as bronze axes and gold. Burial sites of this period have been found on Waddington Fell. At Bleasdale, a bleak and isolated site encircled on three sides by hills, a small community had its dwellings within a palisade of oak posts that had been driven into a clayey soil. Here was a wood circle, in deciduous woodland, complete with a stone-lined chamber in which the cremated dead were laid. A barbed arrowhead, fashioned of stone, was found in modern times.

Fragments of Bronze-Age pottery had been left in the Fairy Holes near Whitewell. An axe-head of the early Bronze Age was located near Blacko

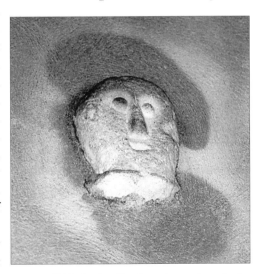

17 *Celtic head, affixed to the north wall of Slaidburn church.*

Tower and a socketed axe of the late Bronze Age was turned up in a garden at Rimington. In 1977 several urns used for cremation were unearthed at Ribchester. Early families doubtless followed game-tracks through wooded areas. Initially, they would clear suitable land using a slash-and-burn technique, such efforts leading to farming and to settlements. Celtic associations include the names of northern rivers – Hodder, Wyre and Lune. A Celtic head, in stone, affixed to the north wall of Slaidburn church, may have been an attempt to Christianise a pagan symbol.

Romans

The Romans, advancing swiftly up the country, encountered the Brigantes, a confederation of Iron-Age tribes who had an orderly life in well-placed, interconnected settlements. A gold bracelet and tress ring of Irish workmanship was found during the laying of a water pipeline at Portfield Hill, Whalley. A hoard of almost 1,000 coins of the Roman period was unearthed near Downham. Evidence of Roman activity at Whalley came to light when Roman coins were found by grave-diggers. A stone head that may have been associated with a native cult appeared at Ribchester, where a Roman fort with the cumbersome name of Bremetennacum Veteranorum ('walled settlement by the Ribble') covered almost six acres and had been used by the natives. Bronze-Age settlement was implied by the discovery of a related sword. Evidence of Iron-Age occupation was afforded by brooches of the period.

Ribchester held a cavalry troop of some 500 men and their steeds, initially a unit raised in northern Spain and subsequently one from Rumania. A spectacular find was a cavalry parade helmet, complete with masks. A temple to Septimus Severus was among the notable buildings. The importance of this fort arose from a convenient river crossing and because it stood at a junction of the road leading through Ilkley to York with another connecting Ribchester to the fort at Overburrow, in the valley of the Lune. This second road, which has been dated to A.D. 79, traversed Jeffrey Hill on Longridge Fell and forked towards the Hodder, crossing it below Doeford Bridge.

18   *Roman altar seen at Ribchester by Pennant, 1801.*

The Rev. Richard Rauthmell, an 18th-century Bowland cleric who described the Roman antiquities of Overborough, stated, 'This military way enters Yorkshire a little below Dowford [Doeford] bridge and proceeds on a direct line on the north side of Newton and Slaidburn through Crossa Greet. It is very apparent on the north side of Tatham Chapel.' Rauthmell describes what he saw when ploughing near Doeford bridge exposed a 300-yard stretch of Roman road. The foundation was seven yards wide and consisted of pebbly gravel 'in order to drain the soft and morassy soil'. The road itself was of large flat stones that came to light when a stretch of road by

19 *Ancient head of a stone cross at Great Mitton.*

Doeford bridge was excavated. Not far from the road, Rauthmell found mounds containing urns. He was aware that the Romans invariably buried their dead by the road.

Angles

In the sixth or early seventh centuries the Anglian kingdom of Northumbria was established 'twixt Humber and Forth. Some heeded the words of their king at York that they should 'go west … take the land, cultivate it, make homes, found villages'. An energetic, lowland people, they have left few details of their occupation beyond the names of settlements. Many of the place-names in Bowland have their origins in the Anglian period. The suffixes *tun*, *ham* and *ing* all mean homestead or farm. They used the term *clough* for a water-carved valley, and *croft* for a small enclosure.

The Angles broke up the stiff land of Bowland using oxen and heavy plough. Free-draining limestone areas, such as at Whitewell and Slaidburn, were made to grow lush herbage for their livestock. Names of notable men have come down to us in folk-tales. Orm, a principal lord, settled on the limestone knoll and his habitation would burgeon into the town of Clitheroe. The nearby settlement of Waddington, an Anglian name, possible indicated a 'town by the wooded hill'. Waddington has been romantically associated with a warrior called Wadda, who settled hereabouts after the Battle of Billington in A.D. 796. The hall named Waddow, a mile out of Clitheroe on the Waddington road, reputedly stands on the site of his camp.

John Waddington, who restored the Old Hall and gave freely to the church, was obsessed with Wadda (also known as Wade), believing that he was descended from this chieftain. It was claimed that Waddington had been Wadetun, 'the town of Wade', and that an offspring named Eigel, a notable archer, shot an apple from the head of his son, centuries before the feat was attributed to William Tell. Chipping, which means 'market', not only existed in Anglian times but was probably the market town for a wide area of Bowland.

Christian missionaries may have reached the district with the Anglian intrusion from Northumbria in A.D. 613, or through converts in Mercia, which became a dominant force in Lancashire south of the Ribble from A.D. 633. Missionaries from Ireland, landing at Heysham in A.D. 640, were noted for their evangelising zeal. Crosses were raised as focal points for preaching, as at Whalley, to be supplemented by churches of wood and thatch. At Slaidburn, the 'Angel Stone', bearing what appears to be the carving of an angel and possibly part of a cross shaft, may have predated the first known church.

Norsefolk

The Norse-Irish who arrived from the west somewhat later than A.D. 900 were generations removed from their Scandinavian forebears, having colonised parts of Ireland and the Isle of Man. Some of the Norsemen may have secured red-haired Irish brides. In the north-west of England they settled with their sheep and other livestock as small family units on land that was not suitable for growing corn and had therefore been ignored by the Angles.

The landscape is rich in names of Norse origin, including *fell* and *dale*, *crag* and *moss*, *beck* [stream], *gil* [ravine], *slack* [hollow], *garth* [enclosure], *keld* [spring or well] and *laithe* [barn], this name being commonly found at almost every moor-edge farm between Slaidburn and the Cross o' Greet. The names of important Norse landowners endure in some names, an example being *Batheraghes* or 'Bathar's hill farm', near Dunsop Bridge. Economy in the use of words eventually cut the name down to 'Beatrix'. The name Bleasdale is said to be derived from the Old Norse *blesa*, meaning blaze or light spot. Anglian names, though, predominate in Bowland as a whole.

20   *Ancient cross in Whalley churchyard.*

21 *Clitheroe Castle, as portrayed in the fourth edition of Whitaker's* History of Whalley.

Normans

Before the arrival of the Normans, land between Ribble and Mersey formed the royal estate of Edward the Confessor. Domesday Book, compiled in 1086, did not define the Forest of Bowland as such, being a record of land then in use. Earl Tostig, a major overlord, had his manor at Gretlintone (Grindleton), where the Norman scribes recorded 38 carucates of land. A carucate was a farmed area for which eight oxen was the requisite team. On the Bowland clays the acreage would be lower than the northern average of 120 acres.

When Norman rule began the valleys of Ribble and Hodder were already well settled, with evidence for the nuclei of many villages. William de Percy, who had arrived on the scene in 1067, was awarded a hundred Yorkshire manors, including Gisburn and Bolton-by-Bowland. Yorkshire territory was subsequently known as Great Bowland. Chipping – the Chipenden of Domesday Book – was not counted with Bowland until early in the 12th century, becoming part of the Lancashire share, otherwise called Little Bowland. The Bleasdale area, although not mentioned in the Domesday survey, was held by Tostig and included in the Forest of Lancaster. As such it was royal property.

A grateful Conqueror bestowed a vast tract on Roger de Poitou, Domesday Book recording that he held the manor of Grindleton and many townships. Roger granted to Robert de Lacy or Lascy the Hundred of Blackburn, the Forest of Bowland and the manor of Slaidburn. The Norman presence was made evident

22 *Insignia of Henry de Lacy.*

by the erection of a timber tower on a knoll at *Cled*-dwr, the future Clitheroe, near where was the Edisford crossing of the Ribble. The tower was replaced in 1150 by a stone keep of modest size, the smallest in the land.

The de Lacys, whose emblem was three luces (pikes), had their principal castle at Pontefract but were benevolent to their outlying territories. Henry de Lacy, who gave Clitheroe its first charter in 1177, died in the Holy Land. Another Henry, Earl of Lincoln, awarded Clitheroe a second charter in 1283. From Clitheroe Castle was administered the Forest of Pendle, which lay within the Blackburn Hundred and was coterminous with the original boundaries of the Honour of Clitheroe as granted to the de Lacys. In the 13th century the road to Pontefract carried a rich and varied traffic of people and animals. Two items plucked from accounts studied in detail by Mary Briggs concern traffic between Pendle and Pontefract. Two stallions from Ightenhill, at the southern part of the Forest of Pendle, were led there by grooms and the same route was traversed by men with 'three and a half stags and twelve does'. A record shows the transportation of the earl's bed to the de Lacy estate in Denbigh.

The de Lacy connection, generally a time of progress, ended with the death of Henry in 1311. His two sons had predeceased him so the honour passed to Henry's daughter, Alesia (Alice), aged twenty-eight. She was married to Thomas Plantagenet, the 30-year-old Earl of Lancaster and grandson of Henry III. Henceforth the castle formed part of the Duchy of Lancaster.

Scottish Raids

Lawless days followed the defeat of Edward II by the Scots at Bannockburn in 1314. Subsequently the north country suffered from fast-moving Scottish raiders who slew people, stole livestock and put buildings to the torch. One incursion saw the Scots sweeping down the Cumbrian coast. They crossed the sands of the rivers Leven and Kent at low tide and rounded up cattle in the Fylde as far as Chorley. They then turned their attention to the cattle-ranches in Rossendale, Pendle, Bowland, Bleasdale and Quernmoor. Chipping was ravaged. In a

23 *Clitheroe Castle and Pendle Hill, from Pennant's Tour of 1801.*

subsequent period of lawlessness and weak government, the constable of Skipton Castle and accomplices raided the Pendle area, gathering up horses and cattle.

Thomas, Earl of Lancaster, led the barons against his cousin, the king, but his cause was lost in battle at Boroughbridge. Found guilty of treason, he was executed at his castle of Pontefract. In the subsequent unrest and civil disorder, the Forest Law was ignored. Stock and game were plundered. Not until the early 1320s was normality restored. Alice, widow of Thomas, was provided with a dower. On the death of Edward II the chases of Blackburn Hundred and of Bowland were granted to his dowager queen, Isabella, for life. In the early 1330s orders were given for the arrest and imprisonment at Clitheroe of those who had trespassed in her parks and had pursued and stolen her deer.

Pestilence and Warfare

Chipping was so badly affected by the plague in 1422 that 'the most grievous desolation reigned where late was plenty'. Bubonic plague, commonly known as the Black Death, raged from 1349 for the best part of a century, affecting the towns more than rural settlements. When, in 1415, English troops engaged the French at Agincourt, their force included men from Bowland, each carrying a type of pike known as a 'bill'. A ballad noted: 'When our foresters struck, death follow'd each wound/The steed and his rider alike bit the ground./There was

24   *Battered keep of Clitheroe Castle.*

glory for England on Agincourt's day/ But the Billmen of Bowland the palm bore away.'

The so-called Wars of the Roses, a protracted and tedious affair for ordinary people, was in essence a squabble between two rival families, those of York and Lancaster, the Lancastrians being particularly strong in Yorkshire. Bowland had its own family feuds. There was bad blood between the Talbots (Yorkists) and the Singletons (Lancastrians) over a hundred Singletons attacking Bashall Hall. The Talbots retaliated in 1469 and poor Alice Singleton died on being struck by lance (price sixpence), arrow and stick. When the offenders were brought to law, the Yorkists produced the king's pardon and went free.

In 1465 Henry VI escaped from Hexham with three of his henchmen before his Lancastrian forces were defeated. The henchmen were captured 'clothed in gowns of blue velvet'. One man carried Henry's Cap of State, which was embroidered with two crowns of gold and ornamented with pearls. While staying at Bolton Hall, the seat of Ralph de Pudsay, Henry took a great interest in the design of a new church. He may possibly have influenced its construction for the elegant and lofty tower, untypical of Bowland, has been compared with that of churches in Somerset, a county well known to the king. Henry was captured by the Talbots when, having dined with the Tempests in Waddington, he was negotiating the stepping stones at Brungerley.

The Civil War retarded progress. At its end, rebellious militia took possession of Clitheroe Castle but quietly dispersed when threatened by General John Lambert. The resistance they had shown led to an order for the Castle 'to be put into such a condition that it might neither be a charge to the Commonwealth to keep it, nor a danger to have it kept against them'. The upper parts of the walls were removed. Holes were blown in the keep. The few guns that remained were taken out of the castle and despatched to Liverpool.

At the Restoration, Charles II conferred the Forest of Bowland on General George Monk, Duke of Albemarle. Monk's son, Christopher, died without issue. The Castle and Honour of Clitheroe came into the possession of the Montagu family.

Three

THE MONASTIC PERIOD

Gifts to the Monks

Early in the 12th century, a time of spiritual renaissance, small groups of monks of the Cistercian order, with grants from the well-to-do, settled in remote, undeveloped areas of the northern Dale Country and, untrammelled by the demands of the manorial system, lived frugally. Ailred of Rievaulx, in Yorkshire, the nucleus from which several other northern abbeys were colonised, described the lot of the pioneers. They drank from a stream. Under their tired limbs there was but a hard mat and 'when sleep is sweetest we must rise at the bell's bidding' yet, 'everywhere peace, everywhere serenity and a marvellous freedom from the tumult of the world'.

At a Cistercian abbey formal worship took place seven times a day. There was but one (meatless) meal. As Norman lords and their ladies heaped more gifts of land on them, a regard for Mammon began to compete with the worship of God. Having achieved satisfying lives in this world, noblemen and women craved an equally delectable Hereafter, which might be achieved through having their souls commended in daily prayers offered by grateful monks. Some donors achieved the ultimate of having their remains laid to rest in abbey grounds.

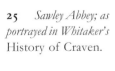

25   *Sawley Abbey; as portrayed in Whitaker's* History of Craven.

26   *Insignia of Whalley Abbey, from Whitaker's* History of Craven.

The money that financed a Cistercian building frenzy came mainly from sheep-rearing. The Cistercian 'white' habit was, in fact, undyed wool, with black scapular – a sort of cloak – and a black girdle. Untutored lay brothers, who did most of the manual work, wore habits of a darker hue. Finding they had a surplus of wool, the Cistercians began to export quality English fleeces to weavers on the Continent. The successors of monks who had resorted to wild places to regain their evangelical zeal through poverty acquired worldly aspirations.

In 1180 Robert de Lacy, last of the original line, granted to the monks of Kirkstall 'all Ristune in Bochland, together with pasture for eight score mares and their foals up to two years and two hundred cows with their offspring up to three years'. Robert's generosity was acknowledged when he was laid to rest at Kirkstall Abbey. Further grants of land from his family, in 1220 and 1235, converted Rushton into a considerable estate extending from the upper Hodder valley to the watershed with the Wenning and the adjacent fees of William de Mowbray and William de Percy. The abbot of Kirkstall possessed a 'Horseclose at Woodhows in Slayborn' and received 20 cart loads of hay annually from the Hammertons.

Sawley and Whalley Abbeys

Sawley or Sally, the westernmost of the Cistercian abbeys in Yorkshire, took its name from 'field of sallows [willows]'. The Coucher Book records that 'in the year of the Lord's incarnation 1147 on the Kalend of January, the convent was sent out, with the Abbot Benedict, to establish the Abbey of Salleia; that noble man, William de Percy, requesting them and preparing a place for them, the 8th Ides of January. It was founded that day, on the first day of the moon.' The journey of Benedict, 12 monks and 10 lay brothers had begun at Newminster Abbey in Northumberland in the latter part of the year 1146. The migrant monks stopped en route at Fountains, in the valley of the Skell near Ripon. Arriving at Sawley, in Ribblesdale, they discovered that William de Percy had set up a timber building for them. It was slowly converted into a stone structure, the main walls consisting of a core of rubble faced by local sandstone.

27 *Whalley Abbey and the Calder, from Whitaker's* History of Whalley.

28 *Detail of Whalley Abbey, from Whitaker's* History of Whalley.

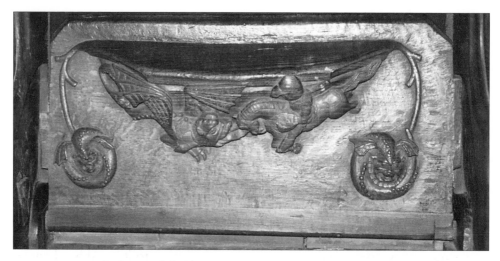

29 *St George and the Dragon, featured on a medieval misericord at Whalley.*

Monks who had lived in the drier eastern areas found the climate at Sawley abysmal. The air was 'ungenial', with excessive rain and fog. When standing crops were almost ready to be harvested, 'they ordinarily rot in the stalk'. The monks were often hungry. To ease their plight, Henry de Percy offered them the valuable church revenues and appurtenances of Gargrave. A petition was sent to Rome seeking paper confirmation of this gift. His Holiness was informed that Sawley stood in 'the most castaway and remote parts of all our kingdom, towards the Irish sea and moreover in a country wonderfully hilly'. Storms, barren acres and aggressive Scotsmen beset the abbey. Consequently, there was not much largess available when needy and helpless people called at the gates. The Pope confirmed the gift of Gargrave in 1321, but Sawley was not noted for its generosity to those in need.

In its prime, Sawley had fewer than 30 monks and novices, with 45 servants. The house-book of 1381 noted that 155 quarters of corn had been used for bread-making. The abbey horses consumed 139 quarters of oats. Each year 255 quarters of malted oats and barley were brewed, which meant that each member of the community drank about 300 gallons a year. The 45 servants included the convent cook (paid a total of 14s. 8d.), tailor (10s.) and poultry keeper (2s.). The amount spent on charity was a modest 5s. 8d. For Sawley, the halcyon days ended in 1175 when another Cistercian abbey was established at Whalley, a few miles downriver.

30 *Stone coffin, Sawley Abbey, drawn by Charles Haworth.*

The newcomers to Whalley had previously been granted land at Stanlaw, on the Cheshire side of the Mersey. They suffered not so much from the weather as from tidal flooding. Hence the gift of Whalley by Henry de Lacy in 1283. There was no haste to remove to their new home. Thirteen years elapsed before a score of monks, led by Abbot Gregory, effected the transfer, taking with them the bones of the ancestors of the benevolent Henry de Lacy. Whalley had several advantages over Sawley, including first pick of salmon on a spawning run to gravel beds in the headwaters of the river. The Whalley community, by competing for local produce – grain, butter, cheese, iron and salt – caused the price of raw materials to rise. A man who sold bark to Sawley raised his price on hearing that Whalley was about to open a tannery.

In the 14th century, when bodies of the dead from the whole of Bowland were interred at the mother church of Whalley, a chapel existed in the remote Brennand Valley. 'Brennand chappelle', the name given to it by Abbot Lyndley of Whalley Abbey in about 1347, had an adjacent shelter. It is surmised that they were available for weary travellers who were half-way along a journey between Clitheroe and Lancaster.

Dissolution

Sawley Abbey was already in decline when Henry VIII adopted Protestantism, arranging for the monasteries to be dissolved. In May 1536 the King's Commissioners paid off the monks. Eighteen received 20 shillings and the remainder had to be content with 10 shillings. One of the Commissioners was Sir Richard Sherburne, of Stonyhurst, Deputy Lieutenant of Lancashire and Master Forester of Bowland; he managed to stay in the good books of four successive monarchs with widely divergent religious views.

William Trafford, the last abbot of Sawley, and two of his monks, and John Paslew, abbot of Whalley, were implicated in a northern rebellion that became known as the Pilgrimage of Grace, a vainglorious objection by the north to the Dissolution. A monk of Sawley composed a hymn that began 'Christ crucified/For Thy woundes wide/Us Commons guide/That pilgrims be.' Trafford was hanged at Lancaster on 10 March 1537. Sir Stephen Hammerton and Nicholas Tempest were hanged, drawn and

31   *Western Gateway, Whalley Abbey, drawn by Charles Haworth.*

32 *North-eastern Gateway, Whalley Abbey, drawn by Charles Haworth.*

quartered for complicity. (The Hammerton fortunes dipped, never to recover.)

Sawley Abbey's oak screen was installed in the old church of Mitton. Sawley Abbey and its Yorkshire lands were granted to Sir Arthur D'Arcy, who had been loyal to the king, and they remained in his family for almost two centuries. William Dobson, author of *Rambles by the Ribble* (1864), left us a sad commentary on the demise of Sawley Abbey. John Harland of Manchester, 'one of the most accomplished antiquaries in Lancashire', while excavating here, found a great number of sculptured stones.

> In the midst of the enclosure is a vast heap of these fragments, many of them being very fresh. Some bear the arms of the Percies, the Tempests or other ancient territorial magnates of the district; others have been portions of pinnacles or parts of groined ceilings; here and there is part of a niche; now and again a broken request for a prayer; the whole being a melancholy commentary on the fleeting character of earthly grandeur.

Leaving the ruins, and walking towards the village inn, Dobson found two arches had been placed across the road. Though of modern construction, they had evidently been built from the ruins. Sculpted stones had been fitted at random 'and not in the best taste; indeed, not always the right side up … In a niche is a broken statue of the virgin, with the inscription, in Latin, in black letter, "Holy Mary, pray for us".'

Much of Whalley land was acquired by John Bradyll of Brockhall, who had acted as bailiff during the Dissolution, and by Richard Assheton of Lever near Bolton, a wealthy lawyer who had purchased the Manor of Downham and other properties. Into Assheton's hands came the site and what remained of the abbey buildings.

The choir stalls in Whalley church were brought here from the abbey church. With them were misericords or 'mercy seats' dating from about 1430. These shallow ledges in the stalls gave the monks a slight concession to comfort during lengthy services. They might appear to be standing but were in fact half-seated. Carvings on the misericords included a woman, asleep while a fox makes away with a goose, and, elsewhere, a seat featuring a blacksmith who is trying to shoe a goose.

Four

FOREST LORE

Bowland was a royal forest in which a king never hunted. The sporting rights were delegated to his friends. E. R. Cunliffe Shaw, chronicler of the Lancashire forests, wrote, 'A forest or chase implied a preserve for red and fallow deer and roe, wild boar together with the lesser beasts of warren, such as hares, foxes, rabbits, cats, martins … and eyries of hawks.' Deer were hunted for sport and also for food. Fresh, lean venison, 'protein on the hoof', was a desirable alternative to meat of indeterminate age that had been salted down for winter consumption. The hawks, taken as young from the nest, met the Norman passion for falconry.

John Lindley, abbot of Whalley, visiting Chipping in the 14th century when the locals were 'few, intractable and wild', mentioned 'a multitude of foxes and destructive beasts'. He concluded that the area was 'in a manner inaccessible to man'. Whitaker, in his *History of Whalley*, copied details of the boundaries of the Forest of Bowland from a document of the early 17th century. It approximated with the perambulation of the forest of 1483 that was quoted by Smith in his *History of Chipping*.

Mainly natural features defined it. From Chipping, the boundary went southwards to the River Loud, thence to the Hodder, Ribble and Bolton Brook. It ran northwards through what is now known as Gisburn Forest to Austwick Common, thence to the skyline feature of Bowland Knotts. The boundary now extended to the Cross o'Greet, a marker at the headwaters of the Hodder, then curled around the heads of Whitendale and Brennand to the Trough, from which it ran to Langdale Head and Burnslack. From here it extended southwards to Chipping, where the circuit was completed. Bowland was abutted by other forests – by Wyresdale to the north-west and Bleasdale to the south-west. Lying to the north of Wyresdale were the smaller tracts of Quernmore and Roeburndale.

Administration

In 1274 Bowland Forest was divided for sporting and some other purposes into four wards – 'Sclatbournewarde' (Slaidburn), 'Baxhofwarde' (Bashall), 'Chepynwarde' (Chipping) and 'Harropwarde' (Harrop). Each ward had a Keeper and helpers who, though spread over a wide area, did their best to deter poachers and those who felled timber illegally. Offences were listed under three headings:

33 *Edisford Bridge over the Ribble, Clitheroe, from Whitaker's* History of Whalley.

against the person, against 'vert' (trees or turf) and against 'venison' (game, mainly deer). A right of 'estovers' covered the use domestically of any dry and fallen wood. Happily for the welfare of wooded areas, many Bowland families cooked or warmed their homes with moorland peat, cut and dried on the moors in summer.

Of the forest courts, Col. Parker mentioned the 'halmote' (chief court) held at Slaidburn, but occasionally in the old days at Waddington. The 'woodmote' (preliminary hearing) took place at Burholme and later at Whitewell, where stood the manor house and a forest chapel. Offenders might be referred to the 'swainmote', where 'verderers', plus a jury of 12 swains or freeholders, fixed the penalties, usually fines. For many years the court rolls reposed in an oak chest at the 'Hark to Bounty', Slaidburn.

The Master Forester, a Crown appointee, was usually drawn from a notable family. He left the day-to-day running of the forest to his deputy, who was known as the Bowbearer. Walter de Urswyk, Bowbearer from 1372 until 1413, was probably the man who arranged for the free-ranging Bowland deer to be emparked at Radholme and Leagram. Walter's manor house at Whitewell stood near the aforementioned chapel, a thatched structure that was re-thatched in 1422. Walter's successors during the 15th century included some notable men – Henry Hoghton, Kt, Thomas Hoghton, Thomas Tunstall, William Assheton, the Earl of Warwick, Duke of Gloucester, James Harrington, Kt and Lord

Monteagle. In the 16th century some of the Master Foresters – Tempest, Clifford, Sherburne – were knights of the realm who leased much of the property. They curbed disputes that involved arms, such as bows and arrows, swords and bucklers. From the middle of the 16th century the Bowbearers were Parkers of Browsholme.

Timber

The glories of the Wildwood were hinted at by the massive blackened stumps of trees dug out of mossland near Chipping and by such names as Stapleoak and Root Farm. The quality of the timber declined with the passing years. A survey within Bowland Forest in 1556 revealed 710 'timber trees being sapplyings', 524 'sapling stubbs', 93 ashes (ash trees) and 500 'samplings on the east and south sides of the lees, and within the office of Alan Bradley.' Two hundred were 'very small trees and shaken and not worth one with another more than 12d each'. The other 300 were 'building timber, but not very large nor clean by reason of the great decay there in times past in delivering out the best trees first, so they are not worth one with another 2s each'.

The greater part of the 'sapling stubbs' were mostly 'old, rotten and hollow, fit only for firewood'. The rest might be used only for 'yate stoops and yates and silles' of the poorest houses. The old stubs, often 'lopped and cropped', were not worth more than 4d. each. Thirty of the 'ashes' were old, hollow and heavily deer-browsed, the wood being worth about 4d. each. The yew, planted in churchyards as a symbol of immortality, was poisonous to cattle and therefore walled off. Archers needing longbows preferred those made from Spanish yew.

Edward Stanley, who had risen to power since the beginning of Henry VII's reign in 1485, was appointed Master Forester and in 1502 acquired a lease for 20 years on most of the local pastures. Among the names were Gregestonlegh, Faldokeholme, Assheknotte and Dynkley Grene. Stanley also had the Park of Laythegrym (Leagram). His chief agent in the district was Christopher Parker. The timber he acquired included olde hollins (holly), olde heythornes (hawthorn), olde hassilles (hazel), olde crabtrees (crab) and oller wood (alder). Only the alder, which grew copiously in 'carres and marysshes' was considered to be worth anything. A saddler named William Isherwood was fined 'for felling a great alder, three small alders and four hollins'.

A demand for good timber, primarily for building work, robbed the landscape of its former well-wooded state. Sir Thomas Talbot, who became Master Forester in 1550, instructed five of the keepers to fell 346 sapling trees towards the repair of tenants' houses 'according to ancient custom'. During the same period, 147 sapling trees (value 16d.) were removed from the lees, mostly for the repair of houses within Clitheroe Castle. Other trees were needed for the reparation of the lodge of Leagram, for the lodge and pale (fence) of Radam (Radholme), and for mills at Chatburn, Slaidburn, Grindleton and West Bradford.

Deer

Three species of deer – red, fallow, roe – were associated with old-time Bowland. Red deer, a lordly species, filled out its frame with good feeding and much cover. During the autumn rut the stags found their voices and converged on areas occupied by hinds, the dominant stags securing – and attempting to hold – a harem until mating was completed, meanwhile driving off competitors. Fallow deer, of medium size, were introduced in Norman times. In the rut a dominant fallow buck used a tree as a focal point and grunted to attract attention.

Red and fallow deer were eventually confined to parks, from which animals were released for hunting. The fallow was more suited to systematic management than the red deer. Having the deer in a relatively small, secure area was a deterrent to poachers and ensured that the deer did not dine on the cornfields of the tenantry. Roe deer, a small species, secretive and largely nocturnal, did not take kindly to captivity and so were not associated with park life. Roe had their nuptials in summer. A doe, having dropped her kids, was mated by the buck. Delayed implantation of the womb ensured that the next kids would be born a year later, in a time of plenty.

34 *A red deer. Pictured here is a hind in its winter coat.*

35 *Ancient thorns on the line of the boundary of Leagram Park at Chipping.*

In 1524, when Sir Richard Tempest was Master Forester of Bowland, much of his time was occupied by investigating affrays between Keepers and the neighbouring gentry and tenants. Sir Richard Houghton and his servants had 'at divers times within the 1½ years killed in the King's forest of Bowland, without warrant, eleven harts, bucks and does'. On St Wilfrid's Eve, at about 11 o' clock, he had arrived in the forest with 30 men 'and there shot 60 arrows at the King's keepers and with their greyhounds killed 6 or 7 great bucks and "sawers" besides other fawns and does'. Sir Richard explained that he had arranged a course on Chipping Common, adjoining the forest. Two hinds were seen. They fled, followed by the hounds, which were led a mile into the forest. 'The hounds were taken up having killed no deer.'

A census conducted by Commissioners in the Forests of Bowland and Quernmore in 1556

revealed the presence of no more than
'six score and fourteen' red deer and
'seven score and six' of fallow. In the
18th century the numbers had risen,
the venison of Stonyhurst deer being
so highly regarded that bidding was
keen when 100 head were offered for
sale on 12 August 1777.

Deer Parks

Selected areas were known as 'launds',
from the Old French for pastureland.
Fencing-in a beast as strong and agile
as a red or fallow deer, the two
favoured species, was achieved by
digging a ditch and setting an oaken
'pale' on the ridge formed of displaced
earth. The main parks were Radholme
(Yorkshire) and Leagram (Lancashire).

36   *Edmund Parker, Bowbearer of Bowland,*
c.*1790.*

What was called New Launde was an enclosure for deer situated on the opposite
side of the Hodder to Radholme. In winter the diet of the deer was augmented
by tree-trimmings.

On a hunt day a gate would be opened to allow a few deer to escape. Little
was left to chance, the selected hunting ground being isolated using barriers
made of brushwood. A drive began, with men and specially trained hounds
directing the deer to where they would become entangled in nets and slain.
Robert Shaw, of New Laund, Whitewell, the last keeper in Bowland Forest, was
appointed to the post in 1774 and held the position up to his death in 1804. In
the following year the last herd of deer was destroyed.

Leagram Park, adjacent to Chipping, lay mainly in low country but was well-
sheltered by fells. It extended to 1,400 acres and was bordered by ditches 8ft.
wide and 4½ft. deep. White thorns (hawthorns) were planted in three rows. A
pallister was occupied full-time, the fence of oak extending to over six and a half
miles. In 1322 the Master Forester of Bolland 'paid for obtaining 300 rails for the
repair of the Launde in Laythgrime park, 100 at 12d. ... 3s.; for carriage of same,
100 at 12d. ... 3s.' A carpenter, employed for two days repairing the houses of
the Lodge, home of the Keeper, was paid 8d. Richard de Hoghton was appointed
Keeper of Leagram in 1410.

Smith, in his *History of Chipping*, mentioned the Pale, a farmstead lying to the
south of the village. The Pale, as its name implied, marked the limit of Leagram
Park and confirmed what type of fence was in use when deer were confined.
The Marsden family purchased the Pale from the Crown about 1550. When

37 *Stirrup gauge, which restricted the size of dogs kept in Bowland Forest.*

38 *Robert Shaw, last Keeper of the Forest. He died in 1807.*

Richard Marsden died in 1609, he left it to his son Thomas. His inventory included geese. There is no mention of deer, as when 'gentlemen poachers' used crossbows, greyhounds and hand-guns. In 1532 Robert Singleton, of Daub Hall, was accused by Sir Thomas Clifford, Master Forester, of killing a buck in 'Laygryme park'. He was accused of slaying a dozen deer in a night's hunting. In 1558, Thomas Houghton and a large party visited a close called Scolehirst Hey, captured one of the keepers, who was named John Dobson, and killed two great stags.

39 *A Longhorn bull, one of the ancient cattle breeds.*

Leagram, disparked in 1555, came into the possession of Richard Shireburne of Stonyhurst. A royal decree stated that hardly any wild cattle or deer remained and that trees and underwood had been laid waste to keep up the 'pale'. Some of the land was already being farmed. Much later, the site of the Keeper's Lodge was occupied by Leagram Hall, a timber building that was altered in the 16th century and rebuilt in stone in the 1770s. Leagram was included in the Stonyhurst estate inherited by the Weld family. The present hall was re-built in 1822 when George Weld and his family took up residence here.

40 *Browsholme Hall, 1750, home of the Parkers, etching by J. C. Buckler.*

Radholme lay across the river Hodder from Leagram. Situated in the sweet limestone country near Whitewell, Radholme was deer-proofed in a manner similar to Leagram. Edmund Parker became park-keeper, the family surname reflecting their occupation. Edmund's sons, Richard and John, were deputy parkers of Radholme. From 1380 they leased the 'vaccary' of Browsholme, the lease being renewed in 1400.

The name of New Laund deer enclosure is perpetuated by the map reference to New Laund Hill, across the Hodder from Whitewell. Stepping stones enable a person to cross dry-foot in normal conditions. The stepping stones existed in about 1800 judging by an engraving of Whitewell that portrays a farmer using them on his way to Laund House. Deer are seen grazing in New Laund fields.

Vaccaries

Vaccaries evolved from the pre-Conquest cattle farms of the upper valleys, helping to meet the food demands of a steadily growing population and enabling my lord to claim more rent for what had been wasteland. On them were raised long-horned cattle and oxen that would serve as draught animals. (Horses were kept by the well-to-do for hunting or fighting.) In the Forest of Bowland the number of 'vaccaries' rose steadily in number from a mere seven in the year 1258, tenanted by generations of the same families. A.R. Lord mentions the existence of nine 'vaccaries' close to Chipping, these being Hazelhurst, Fairsnape, Brooks, Blindhurst, Burnslack, Dinkling Green, Lickhurst, Greystonley and Fair Oak. About the year 1249, vaccaries in the Forests of Wyresdale and Bleasdale were let out to farm and in 1332 these were yielding an annual rent of £21 11s.

The number of farms in Pendle, where the de Lacys owned the cattle, rose to 11 by the century's end. Initially there were five 'vaccaries' in Pendle, on which were kept over 900 animals – bulls, cows, steers, heifers, yearlings and calves. Gilbert de la Legh was in overall charge. A 'geldherd' removed old or barren cows to a collection centre. Cattle were kept in stockaded areas or they ranged across the local fell. A cowkeeper, who had the care of between 70 or 80 cattle, did not own the stock but simply kept the milk and any dairy products made from it, paying my lord £3 a year for this privilege, a toll known as 'lactage'. As time went by, 'vaccaries' were sub-divided and the stocking rate was increased. Among the cowkeepers were Henry sone [sic] of Kit, William Gougge, Robert Attbrigge and Adam the baker.

41   *The Parker crest on the panel of the High Sheriff's coach.*

R. Cunliffe Shaw, in *The Royal Forest of Lancaster*, scrutinised some of the documents concerning the Forests of Pendle and Rossendale – documents devised by civil servants who communicated in Latin and were excessively fond of 'red-tape'. Around the year 1300, noted Shaw, each manager had to complete an annual return that began with a summary, detailed the total number of cows and bulls, and the number of calves born during the year. From this figure was to be deducted the number of cattle that died through 'murrain' (an infectious disease), the number killed by wolves ('strangled by the wolf' was an expression later used) or stolen. The figure for cattle supplied to the central cattle pool was also deducted, leaving information about the total number of cows and bulls at the year's end.

The tenantry must not molest the deer. Fines were imposed if they were detected using dogs to drive deer from their cornfields without a licence. A dog had to be small enough to pass through a stirrup gauge. In the case of truly big dogs, such as the mastiff, the paw had to be small enough to fit a gauge. It was not unknown for several claws to be removed to accord with this rule. When, in 1507, rent increases were proposed by a commission under Sir Richard Emson, with a promise that the deer would be kept under proper control, the tenants of vaccaries and farms objected. Fresh commissioners were appointed; rent reductions were advised.

42 *Stained glass at Browsholme, believed to have originated at Whalley Abbey.*

Decline

One effect of the Scottish incursion in 1322 was the destabilisation of the vaccary system. To allow time for it to recover, farms were let to tenants for a term of seven years. With a rising population and pressure from farming, the system was again modified. In Pendle, the *booths* became the nuclei of hamlets and villages. What had been launds, associated with deer, became rich pastures for cattle. From 1507, when Bowland was partially deforested, there was an impetus to take in more waste land. By the 17th century many of the tenants had become landowners. In 1665 Harrop Hall belonged to the Moore family, who were 'off-comers' from Suffolk. There followed a sub-division of holdings for the benefit of married children. At Sykes, near the Trough, in 1498, the tenant, Thomas Bond, paid a rental of 53s. 4d. a half year. By 1527 Sykes had been divided into nine separate holdings.

During the next century, as agricultural values increased, hunting decreased. What remained of the old mix of trees was confined to remote areas or the cloughs. Towards the end of the 17th century and early in the 18th century people became increasingly prosperous. Building in stone was a feature of the many farms. In July 1828 a notice issued from Browsholme, home of the Parkers, stated, 'It is the particular request of His Grace the Duke of Buccleuch that all his Tenants should assist, as far as they are able, the Keeper and Bow-bearer of the Forest of Bowland, in preserving the GAME. And are hereby requested to WARN OFF and DISCHARGE every Person that may come on their separate Farms without the WRITTEN LEAVE of His Grace or the Bowbearer.'

Five

PENDLE COUNTRY

Pendle Hill (558m.) has kept its shape and size because a summit layer of gritstone protects the underlying softer rocks from erosion. The name Pendle is a composite, based on *penno*, a Celtic term, and an abbreviated English word for hill. The addition of 'Hill' is superfluous. Beneath the impervious gritstone is shale, with bands of sandstone and limestone. Knolls formed of outcropping limestone are conspicuous features in the Ribble Valley, almost in the shadow of the hill – 'Gerna, Worsaw, Ridge and Crow,/Bellman, Salt Hill and Coplow.' When a prehistoric barrow was opened on Worsaw, human remains were found, possibly those of a chieftain who, it is romantically assumed, had been laid to rest facing Pendle.

A beacon flared on Pendle in times of national emergency and, later, to reflect jubilation. The Council of the North noted that 'the beacon of Sharpe [Sharphaw] in Staincliffe, near Skipton, receiveth light of a beacon in Lancashire called Pendle Beacon near Clitheroe.' In 1887 a thousand people climbed Pendle Hill to watch the lighting of a beacon to mark the jubilee of Queen Victoria. Twenty horses hauled the combustibles to the summit plateau. A beacon blazed to celebrate the ending of the First World War.

When it was proposed to add Pendle Hill to the Forest of Bowland Area of Outstanding Natural Beauty, diehards regarded this as a bureaucratic intrusion. Now the two areas complement each other. From many a Bowland fell, the view southwards includes the bold outline of Pendle Hill. From the rim of Pendle's summit plateau, the fells are seen straddling the northern skyline. E.G.W. Hewlitt wrote that the Ribble Valley marked the boundary between a crowded coal-mining and manufacturing district (on the south) and a thinly populated, coalless farming country (to the north). Kenneth Oldham, a former headmaster of Whitehough Camp School at Barley, commented on Pendle's near kinship with the giant sister peaks of Penyghent and Ingleborough, both of Yorkshire. He felt that surely none would argue with the fact that Pendle's bold outline is more akin to the Pennines than to the Lancastrian scene.

On dull days Pendle looks drab. When the sun shines on what is basically a convex mound the shadow pattern changes by the minute and gives the hill extra character. Stand on Pendle on a sharp day in winter and the cold stings so much you feel that ice crystals are entering the blood stream. Richard James, a parson-poet of the early 17th century, saw Pendle standing 'rownd cop, surveying all ye wilde moore lands'. Harrison Ainsworth, novelist, described the Hill as a 'broad, round, smooth mass'. It may not be quite a mountain when judged by height, but this outpost of Lancashire was 'better than the roughest, craggiest, shaggiest, most sharply-splintered mountain of them all'. Samuel Bamford, beholding Pendle in 1842, saw the great hill 'lying huge and bare like a leviathan reposing amid billows'.

43 *Pendle Hill looms beyond the village of Downham.*

Pendle Hill seems to have its own weather system. Pessimists dolefully announce that if you can see Pendle it's going to rain; if you can't see Pendle it's raining! Local people chanted: 'When Pendle wears a woolly cap/The farmers all may take a nap,/ When Pendle Hill doth wear a hood/Be sure the day will not be good.' To an 18th-century commentator, it was 'a vast black mountain which is the morning weather-glass of the country people'. The mountain oozes water, one point of egress being known as Robin Hood's Well. Three times at least the sides of the hill have burst open through a build-up of water pressure within the shales. Such a happening is called 'brasting', which means bursting or breaking. Camden (1580) commented, 'This mountain is most notorious for the harme that it did not long since to the country lying beneath it, by reason of a mighty deale of water gushing out of it.' Charles Towneley (1669) reported that

> the water gushed out near the top of the hill in such quantities, and so suddenly, that it made a breast a yard high and continued running for about two hours. It grew unfordable in so short a space of time that two persons going to church on horseback, one having passed the place where it took its course, the other, being a little behind, could not pass this torrent. The houses in the village of Worston, at a distance of two miles from the point of eruption, were so completely inundated, that the furniture in the lower rooms was set afloat by the turbid stream.

Jessica Lofthouse, viewing Pendle on a stormy day, saw the hill with 'sombre steely greys and indigo, the cloughs and hollows now shadowed, now lit up by

44   *The Big End of Pendle Hill.*

an errant shaft of light'. Kenneth Oldham led parties of youngsters across Pendle in the most varied conditions. Especially memorable was 8 August 1967, when in the late afternoon a vast 'cumulo nimbus' settled around the hill. For over two hours a thunderstorm ran its frenzied course, until the visible hillside was a white foaming cascade. In contrast was the tumultuous wind that beset a snowy Pendle on 13 March 1969. Kenneth and his little party sheltered behind the trig point, their rucksacks forming a windshield. Flakes of ice grew like wafer biscuits from the lee edges of the trig point and from their hats, eyebrows and clothing.

The writer of a Victorian guidebook urged any reader who followed a prescribed cart track to spare their lungs as much as possible. Dr Spencer Hall, impressed by the 'big-end' of Pendle, considered that anyone who surmounted it deserved to be enrolled as an honorary member of the Alpine Club, adding, 'Ay, but this is a pull-up! What a height it seems; and nearly perpendicular.' The short-winded were recommended to begin the ascent from Clitheroe, making the steady ascent to the Nick of Pendle, followed by a long but not too demanding walk to the summit. Rail travellers disembarked at Chatburn or, south of the hill, at Brierfield, on the East Lancashire Railway, about three miles from the base of the Big End. At the summit plateau the visitor was confronted by bogs, bent (a coarse type of grass) and heather, 'amid which a few sheep found scanty pasturage'. At the Big End, the exhausted walker would sit on what remained of the cairn erected by the gentlemen of the Ordnance Survey. Then, as now, sandwiches were popular fare and a gentleman might reach for 'that pleasant travelling companion', his pocket flask.

Baines, in his *History of Lancashire*, gave a short list of rare plants culled from the works of plant-seekers, including the 17th-century botanist Ray. Among these plants were 'least tway-blade'. Camden, in *Britannia*, recorded the presence of 'clowdesbery' (cloudberry – 'offspring of the clouds'). To Dr Leigh (1700) 'cloud-berries' were fruits of 'pleasant taste and a good anti-scorbutie'. Dobson, in Victorian times, confirmed its presence while not corroborating Leigh's assertion 'in praise of the flavour of its fruit or the medicinal qualities of the latter'. The cloudberry had never been known to blossom locally or to produce fruit. In modern times excitement spreads among naturalists each May when dotterel, rare birds that winter by the Mediterranean, visit Pendle in transit to the 'hills of the North'. It has not been a great hill for grouse within living memory; hard grazing by sheep has robbed the hill of most of the heather.

Hundreds of people stumbled up the hill on midsummer morn to watch the sun rise. On the first Sunday in May, adherents of Nick o' Thung's Charity, revived in 1854, spent a day on the hill, preparing meals, gipsy-style, before a camp-fire. Before starting out, each male member of a party had to show half-a-crown, a box of matches and an ounce of tobacco and was expected to recite correctly: 'Thimblerig Thistlethwaite thievishly thought to thrive through thick and thin by throwing his thimbles about, but he was thwarted and thwacked, thumped and thrashed, by thirty thousand thistles and thorns, for thievishly thinking to thrive through thick and thin by throwing the thimbles about.'

The Scout Cairn, a substantial and well-masoned feature of the summit area, was re-built in 2003 and relocated several metres east of its previous location. The cairn of 1982, marking the 75th anniversary of the Boy Scout movement, had been on a site previously marked on the Ordnance map as 'Pile of Stones'.

Pendle Villages

The Forest stretched from Pendle Hill to Colne, extending to almost 13,000 acres, an area of East Lancashire that in Victorian times was to have a string of textile towns. In 1889 W.H. Burnett wrote, 'towns nestle about the base of Pendle as limpets adhere to a rock or as swallows to the eaves of a building. From time immemorial, around it, and around all great mountain masses, villages and farms have crowded as if for life and warmth. Its sides rain down fatness on the adjoining lands and deep within its crust there are strata, yielding life-giving streams and mineral wealth.'

William Howitt, in his *Rural Rides in England*, told how, in July 1836, a thunderstorm drove him to shelter in a cottage at the foot of Pendle. Here he met two children whose appearance was 'as wild as their speech'. He stood at the cottage door, watching the progress of the storm, when 'the head of some human creature carefully protruded from the doorway of an adjoining shed, and was as suddenly withdrawn on being observed.' He investigated. A small girl, about ten, hid a youngster behind her skirts. Howitt asked the girl if the youngster were a girl. 'She answered "Ne-a". "Was it a boy?" "Ne-a." What in the name of wonder were they then? "We are childer." "Childer." And was the woman in the house their mother? "Nea'a." Who was she then? "Our mam." "Oh, your mam; and do you keep cows in this shed?" "Ne-a." 'What then?' "Be-asts." ' Howitt observed that their only clothing was a sort of little bodice with skirts, made of reddish stuff, and rendered more picturesque by sundry patches of scarlet cloth, no doubt from their mother's old cloak. 'On giving them each a penny, they bounded away with the fleetness and elasticity of young roes.'

Impressive views of the hill are seen from Barley, known as Bareleigh in medieval times, the name implying an infertile lea or meadow. It is from Barley that most visitors ascend the hill, some walking from the village and others using a roadside parking area at higher level. At Roughlee, the old hall – now divided into cottages – was the home of Alice Nutter, one of those incriminated in the celebrated witch trial. Newchurch-in-Pendle, which Jessica Lofthouse called 'a grey hamlet', with its one street going 'up hill and down', was formerly Goldshaw Booth, having evolved from one of the huts that were the homes of shepherds and foresters. Its church dates from 4 October 1544, when the Bishop of Chester consecrated the new church of St Mary. A feature on the tower is said to represent the all-seeing eye of God. The sexton at the time of the Pendle Witches, as recorded in the novel by Harrison Ainsworth, bore the unforgettable name of Zachariah Worms. He told Roger Nowell, the magistrate, and Potts, the clerk, that he dug the grave of 'Mary Baldwin, the miller's dowter of Rough Lee'. She was another victim of Mother Demdike.

45 *Pendle Hill from Whalley New Road.*

Sabden boasted that Pendle had a treacle mine, using the treacle in the weaving of parkin. Higham, one of the linear group of villages on the southern flanks of Pendle Hill, was famous for a company established in 1920 to produce Balloon Juice, its activities being noted regularly – and soberly – in the *Nelson Leader* for over 20 years. Higham, like many another village in the area, had an appreciable number of handloom-weavers who were

46 *Pendle Hill from Barley, prior to 1920.*

superseded by three steam-driven textile mills. With their eventual closure, and the opening of a by-pass in 1968, the village regained something of its rural charm. The name of the *Four Alls Inn*, at Higham, is explained on its sign: The parson prays for all, the king governs all, the soldier fights for all – and the worker pays for all. The building, which dates from the last decade of the 18th century, was the venue of a court leet.

Jonas Moore, who lived in Higham for several years, achieved national fame as a mathematician and international regard as a co-founder of Greenwich Observatory. Charles II appointed John Flamsteed to a new role as Astronomer Royal. Jonas supervised his work at Greenwich. In the Great Room at the Observatory were three clocks. One was made in Lancashire with the help of Richard Towneley. Jonas met the bill for all three instruments. Flamsteed is said to have found the first meridian line (o degrees longitude). The clocks were used to work out the different times over the world. And so Greenwich Mean Time came into being.

On the Ribble side of the hill, and within hearing of the whine and whoosh of the by-pass which was opened in 1971, lies Pendleton, a workaday hamlet that is historically old, for a Bronze-Age urn turned up in 1969. The place rated a mention in Domesday Book. It has been closely associated with the adjacent hamlet of Mearley. Great Mearley Hall and Pendleton Hall are farmhouses now, though at the last-named, for nine generations, lived the de Hoghtons.

Pendle Witches

Sir William Pelham, writing to Lord Conway in 1634, mentioned 'a huge pack of witches' lately discovered in Lancashire. Nineteen had been condemned and at least 60 already discovered. More were being revealed daily. Stories concerning the Lancashire (or Pendle) Witches, who were put on trial in 1612, have endured through the intervention of two men, John Crossley and Harrison Ainsworth. But for them, the story would have ended its days in a musty file. Crossley, a solicitor who became president of the Chetham Society, was involved in reprinting

47 *A romantic idea of the Pendle Witches at Malkin Tower.*

the account of the trial of the witches at Lancaster Castle that was compiled by Thomas Potts, at the request of the Justices. Ainsworth, romantic novelist, son of a partner in Crossley's legal firm, incorporated the story in *The Lancashire Witches*, which became a Victorian best-seller.

Almost all we know about the Lancashire miscreants is derived from Mr Potts' *The Wonderful Discoverie of Witches in the Covntie of Lancaster*. It dealt with 'the Arraignement and Triall of Nineteene notorious WITCHES …'. When it appeared in 1613, dedicated to Sir Thomas Knyvet – who arrested Guy Fawkes in the cellars of Parliament, 1605 – the book was widely distributed as a warning against witchcraft and as a guide to finding evidence for its existence. In the year 1845, when interest in such matters had languished, the book was re-issued under the imprint of the Chetham Society as *The Discovery of Witches*. Harrison Ainsworth's ponderous novel, appearing shortly after the reprint, enhanced the appeal of the story. *The Lancashire Witches* was serialised in *The Sunday Times* in 1848 and for this the author was paid a handsome fee of £1,000. The work was published in volume form during the following year.

Ainsworth (1805-82) was a prolific writer, in the style of Sir Walter Scott. He wrote for sixty years, being described by one wondering critic as 'King of the Historical Potboiler'. His story of strange goings-on in the old Pendle Forest was based on three major sources. One was the record of the aforementioned Potts. Another was a diary kept by Nicholas Assheton, of Downham (which was also to be reprinted by the Chetham Society). The third source was an account at Houghton Tower of the visit of James I. Ainsworth began his work with a short prologue relating the events eighty years before that led to the execution of the last abbot of Whalley. He cleverly interwove the two stories.

In *The Lancashire Witches* the bare account of Thomas Potts gathered the moss of imaginative story-telling. Nicholas cries out in amazement, 'Not believe in witches … Why, Pendle Forest swarms with witches. They burrow into the hillside like rabbits in a warren.' Ainsworth was not writing history. He paid several visits to the Pendle countryside before and during the writing of his story and also met members of the Assheton family. The story was re-jigged to suit his plot. He transformed Alizon Device, the weak-minded, delinquent beggar into a ravishing beauty in love with one of the Asshetons.

Over a century after *The Lancashire Witches*, Robert Neill, while serving with the Royal Navy at a lonely spot on the west coast of Scotland, passed winter evenings pondering the escapades of the Pendle Witches and those who had brought them to trial. What had really happened? In 1950, demobilised and with a teaching job, Neill wrote *Mist over Pendle*, an impressive 135,000-word manuscript. The second publisher to whom it was sent accepted it. When it appeared in the bookshops in 1951 it became an enduring bestseller. In contrast was a booklet published in Burnley. The author, Walter Bennett, cut away fanciful aspects of the story and wrote a straightforward account.

A romantic impression of the witch is of a woman with a beaky nose, clad in black with a tall black hat, who sits astride a besom and flies through a storm-ravaged sky. At other times she cackles to herself as she stirs a noxious liquid in a cauldron. Such images do not fit the miscreants who are collectively known as the Pendle Witches. The men and women who were incriminated under an English law of 1604 for practising witchcraft lived in a superstitious age when almost everyone, from the king downwards, was obsessed with witchcraft. King

48 *Inn sign showing a Pendle Witch – and cat – at Barley.*

James I had a pathological fear of witchcraft that led him to write his book *Daemonology*, which included directions for magistrates on what to look for when tracking them down. This led to a widespread witchhunt and, as you might imagine, many witches were found. Witchcraft was a capital offence, a hanging matter. What hope had such as Demdike and Chattox, who were old, withered, spent and decrepit, when their erratic behaviour led to their classification as witches?

49 *Sign at the* Four Alls Inn, *Higham.*

50   *Roughlee Old Hall, home of Alice Nutter, one of the so-called Pendle Witches.*

For years before the witch trial, rumours circulated in the Pendle area about those who were said to be in league with the devil. A plain man's insurance against evil influences was a charm, or several charms, for the spirits of darkness were many and varied. Rowan wood was recommended to protect stock or property against the attention of harmful crones. A popular charm was a luck-stone, with a hole through the centre, which might be suspended from the neck of a person or, if there were concerns for livestock, from a beam in an outbuilding. Farmers and itinerant traders on the south of Pendle Hill had brief encounters with Demdike, Chattox and their crazed offspring. They were widows who, since the death of their husbands, lived in such poverty they had to beg for food. They were considered to have special powers. It was best to give them a trifle and let them shuffle on their way to the next hapless person, or misfortune would occur. A loved one might suffer violent pains or a valuable cow waste away.

Early in the 17th century, remote, thinly populated Pendle Forest was the haunt of innumerable beggars, rogues or vagabonds. Unemployment had led to destitution. Those who strayed from their parishes into adjacent areas were given a good whipping, or worse, and returned post haste to their homes. The Pendle Witches were not hill folk; they lived in gentler countryside on the south side of the hill. Our knowledge of them is restricted to Mr Potts' report; the rest is supposition. Despite a familiar story told about the 'witch's grave' at Newchurch, it is unlikely to be the last resting place of Alice Nutter, the most distinguished of the so-called witches. Her downfall may have been just another phase in the persecution of Catholics.

Was Crow Hill Cottage, north of Pendle Hill, a home of Demdike, as some supposed? The cottage has a circular 'witch's window'. During alterations to the chimney in the 1890s workmen found a wooden image of a person with nails driven into it. The dwelling of Demdike was generally accepted to be Malkin Tower near Newchurch. Richard James, writing in the 17th century, noted, 'And Malkin Toure, a little cottage where/Reporte makes witches meete to swearr/ Their homage to ye divell, and contrive/The deaths of men and beasts …' When the Chetham Society published Mr Potts' account of the witch trial, it noted, 'the witches' mansion is now, alas, no more. It stood in a field a little elevated on a brow above the building at present called Malkin Tower. The site of the house or cottage is distinctly discernible, and fragments of the plaster are still to be found embedded in the boundary wall of the field. The old road to Gisburne [*sic*] ran close to it.'

What might be termed the Pendle Group – for ten others from Lancashire were caught up in the sweep of 1612 – were Chattox (real name Anne Whittle), Elizabeth, Alizon and James Device, Anne Redfern, Alice Nutter, Katherine Hewit, Jane and John Bulcock. The incident that led to the witch trials concerned Elizabeth Whittle, generally known as Bessie, who broke into the 'fire-house' of Malkin Tower early in March 1612. Bessie, who had married John Davies or Device (as written at the trial), pilfered the property of Elizabeth Southern, known as Mother Demdike, who (it was reported) 'dwelt in the Forrest of Pendle,

51 *Good Friday egg-rolling at Barley. Pendle Hill lies beyond.*

a vaste place, fitted for her profession; what shee committed in her time no man knows.' Demdike subsequently died in captivity. Bessie's haul was 'all or most of their linen clothes, half a peck of cut oatmeal and a quantity of meal, all worth twenty shillings and more'. Unwisely, she wore some of the clothes on the following Sunday. A 'band and coif' was recognised and the information passed to the Greave of Pendle Forest.

He informed the magistrate, Roger Nowell, 'a very religious, honest gentleman painful in the service of his country', who had a grand residence in Read Hall, between Whalley and Padiham, and a pew in Whalley church that was known as The Cage because of its many vertical bars. Roger had Bessie brought before him and she was committed to gaol at Lancaster, apparently without any effort being made to substantiate the charges. Alizon Device, granddaughter of Demdike, was also incriminated. She had been heading for Trawden Forest on a begging mission when she met a pedlar name John Law. He refused to sell her some pins and was cursed by Alizon. A black dog appeared and was directed to attack the pedlar, who collapsed, paralysed on the left side. When confronted by the magistrate, Alizon confessed to witchcraft. She mentioned some of Demdike's activities, such as being asked to heal a sick cow that died, and cursed Richard Baldwin, after which his daughter became ill and subsequently died.

Alizon, recalling the feud between her family and the Chattox clan, reported that Chattox had turned the ale sour at an inn at Higham. She also bewitched the landlord's son, using a clay image. The son died. Nowell, having studied more claims and counter-claims, confronted Demdike and Chattox, and her

52   *Whit Walk at Higham.*

53   *Post Office at Newchurch, in the late 1920s.*

daughter Anne Redfern. Demdike confessed to performing deeds that were evil. Many years before, the devil had come to her in the shape of a small boy called Tibb when, on her way home, she had reached a stone-pit near Newchurch.

On 3 April 1612 Demdike, Chattox, Alizon and Anne Redfern were sent to Lancaster Castle, following the Trough route. As they languished in Lancaster Castle Demdike died. On Good Friday 20 people gathered at Malkin Tower, the home of Demdike and the Devices. They had a meal of stolen mutton and plotted to blow up Lancaster Castle

54   *Brass band heading a procession at Newchurch, c.1920.*

and free the imprisoned women. Towards the end of April the man sent to investigate the story of the Good Friday meeting visited Malkin Tower and found human bones stolen from graves in Newchurch. He also discovered a clay image. Roger Nowell now summoned James and Jennet Device and their mother Elizabeth. James confessed to causing the death of Anne Towneley, who had accused him of stealing peat. The slow crumbling of a clay image, representing the dead woman, had brought about the death. Jennet, then only nine years old, named those who had attended the Good Friday meeting.

55 *Huntroyd, home of the Starkies, who owned much of Pendle Hill. Engraving from Whitaker's* History of Whalley.

The aforementioned Alice Nutter, of Roughlee, was a devout Catholic. Having had close relatives put to death because they were Catholic priests, she may have maintained her silence to protect others.

Nowell sent the supposed witches to join those who were in custody at Lancaster and the justices set themselves the task of sorting out tangled evidence. Reference was made to the Good Friday meeting which, according to Potts, was attended by 'all the most dangerous, wicked and damnable Witches in the County ...'.

On 20 August huge crowds gathered for the hanging of the Pendle Group. Were they witches? Hardly. Wisefolk? Maybe. In 1845 James Crossley of the Chetham Society, who helped to revive interest in the Pendle Witches, wrote, 'He who visits Pendle may yet find that charms are generally resorted to amongst the lower classes.' He noted that each small hamlet had a peculiar and gifted person – the wiseman and wisewomen. The white witches of our ancestors 'still continue their investigations of truth undisturbed by the rural police or the progress of the schoolmaster'.

One of Dr Johnson's friends, who ascended Pendle Hill seeking Malkin Tower, penned *Apology for Witches*, in which he blamed for their condition the remoteness of their lives and an absence of a religious influence:

> I doe confesse,
> Needs must strainge phantasies poore ould wives possess,
> Who in those deserte mystic moores doe live,
> Hungrie and cold, and scarce see priests to give,
> The ghostlie counsell. Churches farre doe stand,
> In laymen's hands, and chapples have no land,
> To cherish learned curates.

Sylvia Lovat Corbridge quoted these lines in her book *It's an Old Lancashire Custom*. She added,

> If Pendle, tamed by modern motor roads, today retains some of its magic, the mental and physical state of old crones living on its side in the early seventeenth century must have been the ideal breeding ground for the superstitions, hatred and fears of an age in which the King himself could publish a *Daemonologia*, and the great cult of witchcraft sweep across the whole content of Europe.

Six

MEN OF PROPERTY

At the dawn of the 19th century, Thomas Dunham Whitaker, in major works on Whalley and Craven, left us biographical details of notable Bowland and Ribblesdale families. Whitaker, a Norfolk man who studied Civil Law at St John's College, Cambridge, was himself well connected through his marriage to Lucy, who had family links with Ralph Thoresby, the celebrated Leeds historian. Whitaker compiled his history of Whalley between 1797 and 1799. Its success led him in 1801 to begin researching the history of the Craven district. The first of several editions of his *History of Craven* appeared in 1805.

Four years later the Archbishop of Canterbury presented Whitaker with the vicarage of Whalley, which he held until, in 1818, he was inducted as vicar of

Hammerton   Talbot   Lister

Pudsay   Tempest   Sherburne

56 *Coats of arms of some Bowland families.*

57 & 58   *Assheton coat of arms above the hostelry at Downham; and William Assheton of Downham, 1758.*

Blackburn, with the care of a parish of 110,000 souls – over one per cent of the total population of England and Wales. At a time of political and industrial ferment, Whitaker had little sympathy for radical ideas or, indeed, for industrialisation. He died in 1821, having suffered an attack of paralysis in the previous year. According to his amanuensis, the Rev. Samuel James Allen, his death was 'brought on by constant alarm and fatigue during the Radical disturbances'.

Assheton

A view from the home of the Asshetons at Downham takes in Pendle Hill, two-thirds of which belongs to the family. A gate in a high garden wall accesses the church, within which is the chapel where past generations are interred. The hostelry, in an unspoilt village, sports the Assheton coat of arms. It is here, on Rent Days, in November and May, that the tenant farmers are provided with lunch. The Asshetons have provided 11 High Sheriffs for Lancashire and several for Yorkshire, as well as 17 Members of Parliament. The history of this illustrious family goes back to the 12th century, when Orme, the son of Alwood, married Emma, the daughter of Albert de Grelly, who was Baron of Manchester and Lord of the Honour of Clitheroe.

Through the Middle Ages the Asshetons flourished and produced national figures, including Sir Robert, who was in the first Council of Westminster in 1342. He became Chancellor of the Exchequer and was one of Edward III's executors. In the 15th century the first Sir Ralph Assheton of Middleton became Sheriff of Yorkshire for Edward IV and, in the reign of Richard III, the Vice-Constable of England, being the senior law officer. After the Battle of Bosworth he was, surprisingly, pardoned by Henry VII. His second son was the first Ralph Assheton of Great Leaver (now in Bolton). His grandson, Richard, bought the properties of Whalley Abbey in 1553 and Downham from the Dyneley family in 1558. The Asshetons of Leaver sold Great Leaver and settled at Whalley in 1621.

59 *Bust of William II at Downham, 1789.*

During the Civil War Sir Ralph Assheton of Whalley and his distant cousin, Sir Ralph Assheton of Middleton, were both Colonel-Generals responsible for Cromwell's army in Lancashire. Sir Ralph of Whalley died in 1680, having deeply regretted his part in the Civil War. He left Downham, which was the only property that was not entailed, to the son of his cousin who had died in the war for King Charles. So the Downham property came into the hands of Richard Assheton of Cuerdale, near Preston (the great-grandfather seven times removed of the present Lord Clitheroe).

The Asshetons of Whalley died out within another generation and their property was dispersed among a number of daughters, one of whom married Sir Richard Assheton of Middleton. This branch also died out two generations later, leaving further heiresses, so that by the end of the 18th century all the Whalley and Middleton properties had been distributed to various families – the Curzons, Listers, Suffields, Egertons and de Traffords. The property included the white cattle of Whalley, which were spirited away to the Suffields and the Listers of Gisburn.

From 1558, when Downham was purchased, until about 1800, junior members of the Assheton family used Downham Hall. Notable among them was Nicholas Assheton, who kept a diary which, covering a period of 18 months beginning in

1616, dealt amusingly with his sporting accomplishments. The journal indicates that the premier interests of a rural gentleman were hunting (almost anything), church and the ale-house. Nicholas was fond of his drink, admitting that at times he was 'too busy with drink' and 'merrie, very merrie, merrie as Robin Hood'. When Nicholas died, in 1625, the estate reverted to the Asshetons of Whalley.

At the end of the 18th century William Assheton I of Cuerdale decided to move to Downham. (William had two elder brothers called Ralph; both had died in infancy.) William planted the woods and the park and carried out modifications to the Hall. His son, William II, pursued this project, using the services of George Webster of Kendal in 1835 to extend and convert the Jacobean manor house, in which Nicholas had lived, into the Georgian home of today. When the house was being extended, stone was quarried near the top of Pendle Hill. William II had the idea of pumping water from a fine spring in the quarry to supply the village as well as the new house. Later the waterworks were expanded; by 1950 they were supplying water to Worston and Chatburn, including the mill, the original cast-iron pipes being still in use. The price charged for the water was 6d. for 1,000 gallons.

A link with the family past is the Assheton Sermon. When Sir Ralph Assheton of Whalley left Downham to Richard Assheton of Cuerdale he requested in his will that a sermon be preached annually at Downham in his memory on one of two texts concerning the Resurrection. (A similar request was made for a sermon at Whalley in memory of his son, who died in infancy.) The Assheton Sermon takes place on the last Sunday of January. During the last century, records show that the choices of Job and Colossians – the prescribed texts – have been equally popular.

Hammerton

The family was ensconced in the valley of the Hodder early in the 12th century, when Stephen, son of Hugh, gave 20 cartloads of hay to the monks of Kirkstall. Several years later Stephen's brother, Orme, donated two acres of land 'to God and St Nicholas' and 'the house of Edisford and the leprous brethren there for the health of my soul and for the souls of his wife, Avice, brother Stephen, son John and daughter Annabel'. In 1258, Stephen held all Hammerton at a rent of eight shillings. With the failure of the male line of the Knoll family, the Hammertons – through Adam's marriage to Katherine Knoll – succeeded to their lands. By a series of judicious marriages they acquired vast estates, until it was their boast that they might ride from Hammerton all the way to York and remain on their own land. Marriage allied the Hammertons to the Tempests, the Sherburnes, the Asshetons, Plumptons and Middletons.

In 1536 Sir Stephen Hammerton, having joined the Commons in the Pilgrimage of Grace, was attainted of high treason and subsequently hanged and beheaded. His status as a knight meant that he was not drawn and quartered. It was the

60   *Hammerton Hall, near Slaidburn.*

beginning of the end of an ancient family. In that same year, 1537, his son Henry died of grief. Stephen's widow, Elizabeth, dying in the following year, was interred at Slaidburn. There remains today Hammerton Hall and a number of place-names, some near York. Hammerton Hall, updale from Slaidburn, features the Elizabethan 'E' with a gabled wing at either end and a central, full-height gabled porch. The Hall is not as the famous family would remember it. Oliver Brears purchased their building in 1548. When he re-styled it, parts of the early building were incorporated.

King-Wilkinson

Much of the family history is inscribed on the tablets of memorials in Slaidburn church. The Wilkinson family took up residence in the Hodder Valley in 1626, moving from Hellifield Peel, one of the oldest houses in Craven, to Swinshaw, from where, by way of a goodly number of male offspring, the family branched out on a grand scale. (Swinshaw, a most attractive building, was demolished when the reservoir was being created in the 1920s.) William was a common family name. The surname King-Wilkinson was adopted through marriage in the mid-19th century, the family crest featuring unicorns and the motto *Ne Quid Nimis*. This might be translated as 'not too much of anything' – literally, in today's jargon, 'a little of what you fancy does you good.'

The King family had owned much land, mostly at Aysgarth, in Wensleydale. They had an imposing house, Whiteholme, at Slaidburn, the property having been built by King-Birchall. In the early 1800s William and Leonard had town houses in Blackburn and founded a firm of solicitors known as L.&W. Wilkinson. The Aysgarth property was sold off. Dunnow Hall was built in the 1830s for one of the family and his new bride, whose Grand Tour of Europe ended abruptly in Switzerland when the coach-and-four in which they were travelling came to grief, falling over a cliff. The new Mrs Wilkinson was killed by the fall and subsequently none of the family could bring themselves to live at Dunnow.

In the 1880s William King-Wilkinson initiated a major improvement scheme. Welsh roofing-slate was used but Slaidburn remained an unspoilt village. Recurring Christian names were Leonard, William and John. The family estate extended to 2,000 acres, from Newton to Higher Stoneybank, which was a farmstead beside the Tosside road. The King-Wilkinsons gave £100 to buy the silver-plated instruments used by the Slaidburn Band, which periodically toured the district, including Dalehead. Col. L.C. King-Wilkinson was the squire from 1939 until his death in 1979.

Within the close-knit community of Slaidburn neighbours share joys and worries. Among the joyful occasions was the wedding in 1965 of the youngest daughter of the squire and his wife. A farmer's daughter made the cake. Others helped to make the wedding clothes. Five hundred people attended the wedding and those who were not guests turned up to assist with the reception.

Lister

For three centuries the Lister home was at Arnoldsbiggin, between Gisburn and Rimington. The manor of Gisburn had come to them in 1312 when John Lister married Isabel, the daughter of John de Bolton, Bowbearer of Bowland. An inscription over the main door of an imposing house in the main street of Gisburn noted that it was 'builded anno domini 1635 at the cost of Thomas Lister'.

The Listers did not take up residence at Gisburn until 1797, when they moved from Arnoldsbiggin to Lower Hall, beside the Ribble. Thomas Lister (1752-1826) was created Baron Ribblesdale for his patriotic act of raising a troop of yeomanry in a Napoleonic war. His major ambition was to create an estate on which he might ride from Pendle Hill to Malham Tarn without leaving his own property. He was beggared throughout his life by his ambition to do this, living on a small property near Dartmouth and leaving the running of his north-country estate to an attorney called Thomas Starkie. Gisburn was well-maintained. Whitaker, in his *History of Craven* (2nd edition, 1812), wrote, 'On a tract of several miles along the banks of the Ribble, above and below Gisburne-park, have been planted, since the year 1784, 1,200,000 oaks, besides an uncounted number of other trees.'

Thomas, who became the fourth and last Baron Ribblesdale, was born when his family was staying at Fontainebleau. He was brought to Gisburn as an infant but between the ages of three and 16 his home was in the south. Gisburn made a strong appeal. He had a vivid memory of seeing, 'in Gisburne Park', the 'wild white cattle – not their make and shape but the white blocky effect of the herd against the emerald grass of Craven'. This breed was hornless and conspicuously white except for the tips of their noses, which were black. Such cattle, a Victorian writer had heard, were 'rather mischievous, especially when guarding their young, and approached the object of their resentment in a very insidious manner'. They were said to have been descendants of the indigenous breed that roamed the great forests of Lancashire. The Listers had acquired them from Whalley Abbey at the time of the Dissolution. The last of the historic herd died in 1859.

Thomas was educated at Harrow and subsequently joined the Army in 1873, leaving with the rank of Major in 1886. He had a stormy career as a Liberal in the House of Lords at a time when a major issue was Home Rule. He became a Liberal Unionist – to the annoyance of the Clitheroe Liberals – but returned to the Liberal fold in 1892, when Gladstone was once again in power, becoming a Member of the Privy Council. Lord Ribblesdale lost his position as Chief Whip through his objection to Lloyd George's land policy and condemnation of the landowning class. Outside Parliament, Thomas, a great horseman, was keen on sporting activity and especially deer, attracted in part by their medieval associations and ancient lore.

Ribblesdale took up an official task again when Gladstone offered him the post of Master of the Queen's Buckhounds, a position he held from 1892 until 1895. On the first day of Ascot, Thomas donned the dark green coat of Master, left his Ascot home and, riding Curious, his chestnut horse, led the royal procession down the course. A painting by Lord Ribblesdale in 1902 showed him wearing hunting clothes. He and the Ormerod brothers of Wyresdale introduced Japanese sika deer to the area for hunting purposes; they were emparked and selected animals carted to the hunting ground with the hope they would be recovered and returned to the park at the end of the day. Inevitably there were escapees, and a feral population developed.

Lord Ribblesdale was twice married. War robbed him of his two sons. Thomas, his elder son, was killed in Somaliland. Charles joined the Army in 1914. Two years later his body was one of thousands lying on the beaches of Gallipoli. It is recalled that when Lord Ribblesdale heard of the death of his second son, and heir, he rode a pony round and round Gisburne Park until both fell exhausted. He died in October 1925, and was interred in the family vault at Gisburn.

Thomas, 4th Baron Ribblesdale, had been a man of two worlds: of high Victorian society and of a country estate in Yorkshire. An epitaph at Gisburn church describes him as 'a man of many joys, A man of many sorrows, He gave his sons to Death In their country's service, And following them to rest Closed

worthily the course of an ancient and honourable line.' The association between
the Listers and Gisburn ended in 1943. Today the old hall is used as a private
hospital.

Parker

The Parkers of Browsholme, who derived their surname from their ancient role
as keepers of Radholme deer park, were prominent in the life of Yorkshire for
six centuries, up to 1947, when Bowland became part of Lancashire. In their
time, members of the family were High Sheriffs, Deputy Lieutenants and Justices
of the Peace. The family's descent was from Peter de Alcancotes, who in the
mid-13th century held the Manor of Alkincoats, Colne. His great-grandson,
Edmund, became the first park-keeper. The Parkers were Bowbearers, a task for
which they needed administrative ability and a good education. Many of the
family, being graduates of Cambridge, were well-versed in reading, writing,
accountancy and the law.

From 1380 Edmund's sons, Richard and John, leased the vaccary of
Browsholme, this lease being renewed in 1400. They were deputy park-keepers
of Radholme in 1393. When Richard retired with a pension in 1411, his son

Edmund and grandson Giles
succeeded him. Giles, of Horrocksford,
was the tenant of Nether Browsholme
in 1482 and his son, Edmund,
negotiated a new lease of this property
from the Crown in 1507. Edmund
commissioned a grand house, shaped
in the traditional way like a letter H, a
central hall flanked by a parlour wing
to the west and kitchens to the east.
He died in 1547, and in 1603 Thomas
Parker, having bought the freehold of
Browsholme, had the wings and front
of the family mansion re-faced in
sandstone. A fourth storey was added
and the central frontispiece affixed in
a style similar to Stonyhurst, featuring
the three orders of Greek architecture,
Doric, Ionic and Corinthian.

Thomas, having married a
Tempest, bought from that notable
family in 1630 the advowson of
Waddington church. His son, Edward
(1602-67), who succeeded him at

61 *Browsholme Hall, home of the Parkers,
displays three orders of architecture – Doric, Ionic
and Corinthian.*

Browsholme, experienced the trauma of Civil War, despite receiving letters of protection from prominent men on each side. Roundheads removed goods worth over £1,000 and they imprisoned Edward, his seven-year-old son, at Thornton. When, in 1652, a Commonwealth review included the Forest of Bowland, it was assessed that Robert Parker owned 929 acres – and relatively few deer. These were described as 'redd deere of all sorts, viz. Staggs, hyndes and calves 20 – and of fallow deere 40'.

Edward Parker (1730-94), Bowbearer of the Forest of Bowland, aged twenty, married Barbara, daughter and co-heiress of Sir William Fleming, of Rydal Hall, Westmorland. Barbara brought to Browsholme a lock initialled AP (Anne Pembroke, better known as Lady Anne Clifford, who had presented it to the Flemings in 1672). John Parker (1755-97), who also became Bowbearer, married Beatrice Lister, of Gisburne Park. He was a friend of William Gilpin, a celebrated topographer, and accompanied Gilpin on some of his travels.

John's eldest son and successor, Thomas Lister Parker (1779-1858), a patron of the arts, was among the friends of the Prince Regent. In anticipation of a royal visit, he added a whole wing to Browsholme and spent over £100,000 on landscaping the gardens. (The visit did not take place.) Parker's friends included Thomas Dunham Whitaker, cleric and historian, through whom he was to meet the artist Turner, then little known; he had travelled north to make sketches for illustrating Whitaker's *History of Whalley*. Turner's painting of Browsholme Hall became one of the Parker family treasures.

A skull kept in a court cupboard at Browsholme was said to have been that of a martyr in the Pilgrimage of Grace. It was linked in a curious way with strange happenings in the 1850s: sections of the façade of Browsholme fell away; fires broke out from smouldering beams under the great roof; there were sudden deaths in the family. Master Edward Parker, on vacation from Harrow, confessed that for a prank he had taken a skull from a court cupboard and buried it in the garden. The skull was recovered and normality was regained on its return to the house. The Parker family had alternative accommodation for two years while their hall was being repaired. The Parker vault in the chapel on the north side of the chancel at Waddington church was first used for Giles Parker, who died in 1500. The last member of the family to be interred before it was finally sealed was the Rev. John Fleming Parker, vicar of Waddington for fifty years, who died in 1862.

Colonel Parker, who had served in the Parachute Regiment during the Second World War, inherited Browsholme when it was subject to a crippling liability for death duty. A major part of what remained of the estate had to be sold off. He undertook vital repairs with help from the Historic Buildings Council, opening the hall for most of the year and personally conducting visitors through the main rooms. On his death, in 1975, the colonel willed it to his cousin and godson, Robert Redmayne Parker, who at the time, aged 20, was studying to be a land agent. His father, Christopher, executor under the will, administered the estate for some years. Browsholme is open to the public at prescribed times and is the setting for musical events.

Peel

In 1258 the manor of Knowlmere was part of the estates in Newton that belonged to Elias de Knoll. The estate was inherited by his great-granddaughter, came into the possession of the Hammerton family through marriage, and was forfeited to the Crown when Sir Stephen Hammerton took part in the Pilgrimage of Grace. Knowlmere was sold to Robert Parker, in whose family it remained for many generations before coming into the ownership of the Duke of Buccleuch, who sold it to the Peel family.

Knowlmere, a mansion dating from 1848-9, was commissioned by Jonathan Peel, who on 17 November 1849 celebrated by giving a 'a liberal entertainment' at the *Parkers Arms*, Newton, attended by 70 relatives and friends. The mansion – for so it was planned to be – was designed in the Elizabethan style by Arthur Hill Holme, architect of Liverpool, and built by the Clitheroe firm of William Hargreaves & Nephew. An account in the *Preston Guardian* recorded that 'the building covers an area of nearly 600 yards, is built of hewn stone and is now roofed in and covered with slate in the astonishingly short space of 30 weeks'. Visitors were charmed by its many gables and chimneys and by a well-manicured park extending to the river Hodder.

62   *Bolton Hall, home of the Pudsay family.*

63 *An interior view of Pudsay Hall at Bolton-by-Bowland.*

In recent times Judge Peel presided over the estate. The Peel family is still well represented in the Hodder valley and many members of former generations are interred in the churchyard at Slaidburn.

Pudsay

A family association with Bolton-by-Bowland began in 1331. John de Bolton granted to his grandson, John de Pudsay, lands and tenements in the village, enabling a chantry chaplain to be appointed to say mass over a period of 16 years. De Pudsay, who became lord of the manor in 1349, granted a market charter (Wednesday) and authority for a three-day fair to be held each year 'on the vigil, on the day and on the morrow of the Apostles Peter and Paul'. John died in 1365 and was succeeded by his son Henry, who had married Elizabeth Layton. By that marriage the family acquired the manor of Barforth in Teesdale. Henry's son, John, was knighted and fought the French at Agincourt.

Three generations of Pudsays had links through marriage with the influential Hammertons, Tempests and Cliffords. The next three generations acquired glory and renown, their local deeds including the transformation of the parish church from a modest Norman edifice to a splendid church with a tower that stood out from other Craven towers because of its height and degree of adornment. Sir Ralph Pudsay, son of Sir John, who died in 1468, was to be remembered because of the carvings on his tomb in the Pudsay chapel of the church, which is adorned with the figure of the man and his three wives in chronological order, Matilda, Margaret and Edwina, the last-named surviving him. Between them, they had 25 children. Carved on the lower folds of the dress worn by each wife is a figure in Roman numerals representing the number of children she had borne. Some of the children are shown in armour, others dressed as priests.

64   *Tomb of Ralph Pudsay in Bolton-by-Bowland church.*

The base of the tomb having been reduced to rubble during the Civil War, it was renewed by Ralph's descendant and heir, Pudsay Dawson of Hornby Castle, in 1857. On it are portrayed coats of arms marking the descent of Sir Ralph and his second wife, Margaret Tunstall. Sir Ralph was among those ardent supporters of the Lancastrian cause who played host to an English king, Henry VI, after his defeat by the Yorkists at the Battle of Hexham in 1464. In the grounds of Bolton Hall the King used a divining rod to locate water and had a well dug and lined with stone so he might have a cold bath periodically. Subsequently, the well was venerated by the country folk, those who were ill visiting it in the hope that by sipping the water they would be cured of their disabilities.

It has already been suggested that the lofty, much decorated tower of Bolton church, which is similar in some respects to churches in Somerset with which the King was associated, might have been partly inspired by the Pudsay's notable guest. Henry left at Bolton a spoon, a pair of boots of brown Spanish leather, lined with deerskin, tanned with the fur on, and a pair of gloves of the same material and lining. An engraving of them appeared in the *Gentleman's Magazine* for 1785.

The King then moved on to Waddington, where the owner, Sir John Tempest, along with members of the Talbot family from Bashall betrayed him. He managed to escape from the house but was caught as he approached the stepping stones of Brungerley Bridge near Clitheroe and was taken to London. Edward IV rewarded the Tempests and Talbots but misfortune later visited the Talbots. King Henry was not forgotten locally, for at Whalley an altar was dedicated to the 'Blessed Mary and Saint Henry'.

A chapel was added to the church by the Henry Pudsay, who died in January 1520. His son Thomas provided an endowment to pay a chaplain, 'to th'enten to pray for the sowle of the founder and all Christen sowles, and also to say masse at the manor of Bolton, when he shall be required by the said founder and his heirs'. Thomas, imprisoned in York Castle for recusancy, died here in September 1576. His son William, who inherited at the age of 20 and died in 1629, had 14 of his 18 children baptised in the parish church. William is recalled as a counterfeiter, a reputation discussed on p.110. Ambrose, the last of the male line, a lawyer in Leeds, died in 1728 and was interred at Bolton-by-Bowland.

The succession passed to Bridget Pudsay and to Christopher Dawson jointly. Dr Pococke, in 1751, considered Bolton Hall to be the oldest house he had ever seen in England. Bridget died in 1771. The property now came into the hands of John Bolton of Liverpool who, between 1806-8, extended it, having gables built on the west front, rebuilding the south gable and arranging for the front entrance to be on the north side. Meanwhile, the relics of the King's stay at Bolton Hall were taken to Hornby Castle, the residence of Pudsay Dawson, whose heir, Captain Dawson, in 1862 loaned them to South Kensington Museum. In the same exhibition the Hon. Robert Curzon loaned a pen case that had been left by the King at Waddington Hall, where he was betrayed.

William Dobson (1864) recalled Bolton Hall as 'the grey old mansion in its fringe of green woods'. He was permitted to tour the main rooms. In the banqueting hall were 'suits of old armour, huge horns of the elk and of other deer, numerous family tokens and massive old oak furniture'. The hall became infested with dry rot and was damaged by fire; it was demolished in 1959.

65 *Sir Ralph Pudsay and his large family, as portrayed on his tomb, from* Whitaker's History of Craven.

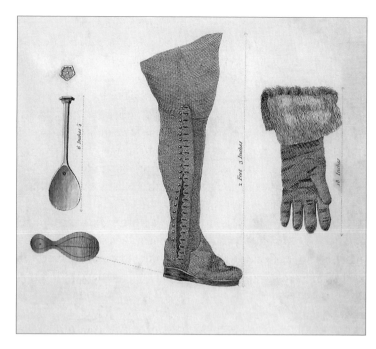

66 *The boot, glove and spoon left at Bolton Hall by Henry VI, as illustrated in Whitaker's* History of Craven.

Sefton

Sefton ('village of the reeds') stands beside the river Alt and was the home of the Molyneux family, who became Earls of Sefton. Their principal house at Croxteth was described as 'a palace within a park'. In the 1880s the Sefton family developed a large estate in Wyresdale and in 1886 built Abbeystead House, which was intended to be a shooting lodge after the style of those that wealthy industrialists were establishing in the hill country of Scotland. Abbeystead was named after a monastic foundation that, after a short time, was transferred to Ireland.

In Wyresdale, the style of the big house, the lodges and Home Farm is vaguely Elizabethan. The Earl used old buildings as the nucleus of an attractive hamlet in a woodland setting. Sandstone quarried on Tarnbrook Fell and transported by horse and cart was used on new building projects. The present owner is the Duke of Westminster. His Abbeystead estate consists of 19,500 acres.

Shireburn or Sherburne

Towards the end of the 13th century Walter de Bayley was given 'the land of the Stanihirst'. In 1372 John de Bayley was licensed to establish an oratory here. Five years later Richard de Bailey of 'Stanihurst' married Margaret Shireburn, daughter and co-heir of Sir Richard, unexpectedly yielding his surname to that of his bride. Thus began a dynasty that was to claim descent from Randulphus le Rus – otherwise Ralph the Red – the red hair persisting in the family for many generations.

Hugh Shireburn, founder in 1523-4 of a short-lived chantry in Mitton church, succeeded to the Stonyhurst estate in 1537 and held it for 57 years. Hugh married Dame Maude, daughter of Richard Bold, and became, according to an inscription on his tomb, 'Knight mast Forster of ye forrest of Bowland, steward of ye Manor of Sladeburne Lieuten of ye Ile of Man'. In 1562 Sir Richard had a bridge built across the Hodder, a structure costing £70 that would become known as Cromwell's Bridge. Around 1590 he began the creation of a grand house at Stonyhurst. He died in July 1594 as work was in hand to create an imposing chapel, where his wife, Dame Maud, was interred. Her effigy, and one of Sir Richard, sculpted in alabaster, was set on a table-top tomb, the sides adorned by armorial bearings.

The Shireburns, like many another old family, suffered through their adherence to the old faith. The Earl of Derby described Lancashire in 1583 as 'this so unbridled and bad an handful of England'. In 1612, the king ordered Justices of the Peace in Lancashire to report anyone who did not take Protestant communion in church. They would be prosecuted. During the Civil War, six members of the Shireburn family died. They were devoted to the last to King and State. Ironically, in 1648, Oliver Cromwell – their chief tormentor – spent a night at the partly-completed Stonyhurst, then described as 'Stanihurst Hall'. The army was quartered in a nearby field.

The Protector described the hall as 'the finest half-house he had ever seen'. Having a dread of assassination, and therefore of strange beds, he slept on a table

67   *The Sherburne Chapel at Great Mitton, from Whitaker's* History of Whalley.

68   *Detail from one of the alabaster tombs in the Sherburne Chapel, Great Mitton.*

that had been drawn to the middle of a room and kept beside him his sword and pistols. One of his captains, named Hodgson, confided in his diary, 'That night we pitched our camp at Stanyares Hall, a Papist's house, one Sherburne's …' Following a dash through the Craven Gap, Cromwell had cut off the Royalist forces. He defeated them near Longridge and revisited Stonyhurst on his return journey to Yorkshire.

Richard, who succeeded to Stonyhurst in 1667-8, built and endowed a school and some alms-houses at Hurst Green. He was arrested in 1689 for Jacobite sympathies and died while in prison at Manchester, his body being taken to Mitton for interment. The eldest son dying without issue, Stonyhurst passed to brother Nicholas, who was to be the last of his ancient name to hold the estate. Sir Nicholas, as he became,

69   *Another detail from an alabaster tomb in Sherburne Chapel.*

raised monuments, laid out the grounds, excavated the long ponds complete with fountains, and set cupolas on prominent turrets. Well-disposed to local people, in 1699 he introduced them, through a skilled teacher, to the spinning of Jersey wool, a satisfying way by which they could augment their income.

Sir Nicholas built almshouses with a chapel on the east end of Longridge Fell. Ten rooms were available for needy folk from prescribed villages on the Shireburn estate. (Much later, the almshouses were rebuilt as workers' cottages in Hurst Green.) Towards the end of the 17th century he beautified the approach to his home. Two great ponds were excavated, gardens were laid out and, being a friend of James II, he probably borrowed the King's 'trusty Beaumont' to design them in the formal Dutch style, with rectangular paths, terraces, steps, statues and fountains to which water flowed through pipes made of hollowed-out tree trunks. His worst investment proved to be the 1,000 yew plants purchased to form a hedge. The cost in 1698 was £16 13s. Nicholas's hopes for the continuing glory of his family ended in 1702 with the death of his young son, Richard Frances – from eating yew berries.

On the death of Sir Nicholas on 16 December 1717, the estate passed to his daughter Mary, who had married the Duke of Norfolk. She died without issue. The Stonyhurst estate passed to Mary's aunt, Elizabeth, wife of William Weld, of Compton Basset in Wiltshire. In 1794 the house was made available to Jesuit Fathers who, with the boys of their school, had to flee from religious intolerance on the continent.

Talbot

Thomas Talbot, who had been the Constable of Clitheroe Castle under the De Lacys, acquired the manor of Bashall early in the 13th century. In the 15th century, when Bowland was still a remote area and the law none too vigorously upheld, family feuds were common and bitterly pursued. A feud between the Talbots and the Singletons of Withgill erupted into violence in 1461, when over a hundred Singletons and their friends attacked Bashall Hall.

Eight years later the Talbots, who might have been bred for war, had their revenge. At Mitton, Alice Singleton was struck by a lance (price sixpence), her assailant being John Talbot, who was described as a gentleman. Alice died instantly. Richard Talbot, gentleman, made sure and 'struck her with an arrow as far as the brain'. Also involved were Thomas Talbot of Bashall and Nicholas Tempest of Bracewell. This was a time when the House of York was in the ascendant, and the Talbots were in the king's favour, having betrayed Henry VI after the Battle of Hexham: 'King Henry was taken in a wode called Cletherwode beside Bungerly hipping stones by Thomas Talbot and Bashall and John Talbot his cosyne of Coilbry ...' The hapless Henry was delivered to the Yorkists and the Tower of London, and Thomas Talbot received £100 and a pension of £40 a year from a grateful Edward IV.

The warlike Talbots kept what was virtually a private army, quartering their retainers in a large building behind their Hall. The Hall has taken its present form from many periods and is surrounded by walled gardens and accessory buildings. In the 17th century the estate passed to two daughters and eventually into the hands of Colonel White, who had married one of them. White, secretary to Sir Thomas Fairfax, was a member of the Long Parliament.

Towneley

This notable family adopted the name De Tunley towards the end of the 13th century. Towneleys were numbered with the Billmen of Bowland in 1415, when many a family found glory 'on Agincourt's plain'. Following the restoration of the monarchy in 1660, Charles II rewarded a principal supporter, General Monk, with the gift of the Royal Forest and Manors in the Honour of Clitheroe; he was also given the title of the Duke of Albemarle. The lands came into the possession of the Duke of Buccleuch. He disposed of the estate. Gradually the property was offered for sale and Peregrine Edward Towneley bought the whole in stages.

On the death of Colonel Charles Towneley in 1876, his brother, Colonel John Towneley (1806-78), became administrator of the Towneley property but did not immediately take up residence at Towneley Hall, Burnley. He and his

70   *A Bowland interior. The Hall at Little Mitton. From Whitaker's* History of Whalley.

family preferred the more secluded Thorneyholme at Dunsop Bridge, a property his father had acquired early in the century. (It was at the Thorneyholme stables that Kettledrum, which won the Derby in 1861, was reared and trained.) John married Lucy Ellen, daughter of Sir Henry Tichborne in 1840. They had one son, Richard Henry, and four daughters, Theresa Harriet, Lucy Evelyn, Mary Elizabeth and Mabel Anne.

On the death of Colonel John, in 1878, the male line of the Towneleys of Towneley ended, the estates being divided between his daughters, Lady Norreys, Lady Lennox and Lady O'Hagan, and his brother. The personal estate was sworn at a figure of under £50,000. The Colonel left money to his servants and gifts of saddle horses to two of his daughters. The remainder of his property passed to his wife, Lucy Ellen, who was to survive him by 12 years, her death occurring in 1900 at her London home in Upper Grosvenor Street. None of John's daughters had any children. (The son, Richard Henry, had died in Italy a year before his father.) Richard and his parents were interred in a family vault at St Hubert's, Dunsop Bridge. The family succession passed on through the female line. One who married a descendant assumed the surname of this illustrious family.

71 *Lord Ribblesdale, the last of his line, lived in style at Gisburn. The painting is by Sargent.*

Wright

The connection between the Wright family and Bowland-by-Bowland began in 1866, when C.B.E. Wright, who was a Doncaster coal-owner, purchased the Bolton Hall estate from Mrs Mary Littledale. His first impulse was to enlarge the house and garden, creating a range of heated orchard houses. A subterranean palm house was entered along a passage lit by acetylene gas. He employed almost one hundred local people, the housekeeper, Miss Humphreys, having had a staff of twenty.

72   *Former* Ribblesdale Arms *at Gisburn, restored for private use.*

Mr Wright had the name of the inn changed from *Windmill* to *Coach and Horses*, after his principal interest. In 1894 he owned about seventy horses, with a groom to every three of them. When he visited London he sent two grooms and four horses to Doncaster and a similar number of grooms and horses to Newark. He then set off, driving his four-in-hand with two grooms occupying the back seats. In the harness room at the Hall stood the skeleton of a horse, with the skeleton of a man leading it. In attendance was the skeleton of a dog.

Mrs Wright (Edith de Cardonnel), who died in 1912 aged 63, was an invalid who, when visiting the village or attending church, travelled in a donkey-hauled carriage in the charge of a groom. The Wright family and members of their staff entered the church through a small door adjacent to the Bolton Hall chapel, which became the Lady Chapel. A plaque was affixed to the wall in memory of Godfrey Charles de Cardonnel, an Army officer killed while leading his men at Diamond Hill, South Africa, on 11 June 1900. Mr Wright died in 1924.

Seven

HEART AND SOUL

Early Churches

Something of the grandeur of Bowland past lingers in the sight of coats of arms incorporated in stained-glass windows at Stoneyhurst, Mitton and Whalley. In Whalley's parish church the arms of 25 local families of distinction have been a feature of the east window since 1816. Carvings on the misericords strike a humorous note. These were in Whalley Abbey until the Dissolution. In a lifesize stone effigy, the historian Whitaker stares fixedly – perhaps even censoriously – across the ecclesiastical greyness of this vast building.

Three stone crosses in the churchyard at Whalley have prompted more questions than answers. Local tradition says that any person who can decipher and transcribe the hieroglyphics on the largest cross will acquire the power to

73 *Effigy of Dr Thomas Dunham Whitaker at Whalley church.*

74   *Medieval font head at St Helen's church, Waddington.*

75   *St Mary's, Newchurch, a focal point of the Pendle country.*

become invisible. Harrison Ainsworth, the novelist, gleefully used this piece of folklore in *The Lancashire Witches*. The tallest cross may have been a copy in stone of a wooden cross that, in its prime, was brightly painted. A stone cross, raised by Irish-Norse settlers of the tenth century, has a central panel featuring a haloed saint between two serpents.

A church existed at Whalley in 628 but the present building dates back to 1206. The first incumbent, Peter de Cestria (1235-96), was a rector. His successors, selected by the abbot of Whalley, were designated vicars. Stalls dated 1430 and inscribed in Latin, French and English were moved here from the abbey church. In its early days the parish of Whalley extended over one-ninth of Lancashire. Before industrialisation on a grand scale elevated small villages into busy towns, the vicar of Whalley was concerned with the well-being of parishioners in the area between the Ribble and Rochdale. Within that parish was a tiny settlement called Burnley and a village known as Marsden that would later blossom under the name of Nelson.

The Old Faith

There is a whiff of antiquity about many of the Bowland and Ribblesdale churches. Mitton, like Whalley, has its most venerable objects in the churchyard. An ancient carving of the crucifixion stands on a relatively modern column. All Hallows'

Church (c.1270) has a superb position on high ground, with Pendle Hill brooding on the horizon. Another church that has retained an air of antiquity is St Andrew's at Slaidburn. As at Mitton, it is not the first church to have occupied its prime site. In the 12th century Hugh de la Val granted the advowson to the Priory of St John of Pomfret. The Norman font, of around 1229, has an oaken cover dating from the Elizabethan period. In the south aisle is the Hammerton Chapel, named after a family who in 1447 enhanced the modest endowment, made by Peter Shawe, to the honour of Our Lady.

Slaidburn's three-decker pulpit was installed in 1740, when high box pews were becoming fashionable. The pews are of various dates in the 17th and 18th centuries, the earliest bearing the date 1616. The clerk, who leads the congregation's responses, uses the lowest stall. The minister occupies the middle stall, then preaches from the top deck. In the churchwardens' accounts at Slaidburn for 1777 appears the item: 'To Peter Winder for mending a whip 4d.' A pair of whips was kept in the church vestry. The dog-whipper, a church official, was paid annually for keeping unruly dogs in order during divine service. He also expelled any strays. The last payment of ten shillings was made in 1863.

A church has existed at Bolton-by-Bowland since 1190. Several times rebuilt, the church of today is largely the product of a major rebuilding in the mid-15th century. Sir Ralph Pudsay, lord of the manor, enlarged the nave, lengthened the chancel and built a lofty tower that in its architecture and decoration is different from the usual Craven church. Heraldic shields commemorating the Pudsay association through marriage with Bankes, Tunstall, Clifford, Tempest, Hamerton and Layton adorn the 16th-century font, which was fashioned of grey marble. Many pews are of late 17th-century date. The Pudsay Chapel, built in the 16th century, is a result of the custom whereby a wealthy family would employ a priest to say mass daily for the souls of its deceased relatives.

Whitewell church, dating from early in the 15th century, is on the site of a thatched place of worship that served the forest folk. They had previously to attend services at the chapel of St Michael in Clitheroe Castle or a small

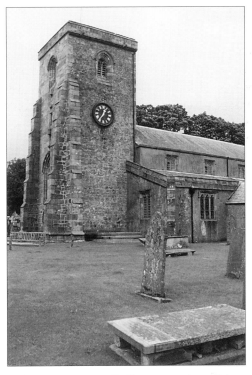

76 *St Andrew's, Slaidburn, on a site used for Christian worship since the 10th century.*

chapel tucked away at the head of the Brennand valley. The 'new church' that gave its name to the Pendle village of Newchurch was a chapel of ease when the Forest was deforested early in the 16th century. St Mary's is one of the few churches holding an annual rushbearing ceremony, originally concerned with replacing stale rushes covering the church floor with rushes that had been freshly cut. Rushes are no longer strewn on the floor but each August a Rushbearing Queen is crowned and a procession through the village ends at the church, where a service of thanksgiving is held. Above the string course on the west wall of the tower, which dates from 1653, is an oval stone incorporating a piece of glass – said to represent the all-seeing eye of God.

77   *The tower of Bolton-by-Bowland church, in a style said to have been influenced by King Henry VI.*

Religious persecution was rife in the 16th century. Catholic families who wished their sons to be brought up in the faith sent them abroad. A Jesuit college founded in St Omer in northern France in 1593 met such hostility from the Bourbons that it moved, first to Bruges and then in 1773 to Liege. In 1794, with the French Revolution raging, the college was moved to Stonyhurst Hall, which at that time was owned by Thomas Weld. He had been a pupil at the college during its time at Bruges. The masters and boys began the journey to their new home on boats down the Meuse. They then sailed from Rotterdam to Hull. A barge conveyed them up the Ouse to Selby, 55 miles as the river wound its way. A canal boat was used from Leeds to Skipton and an 18-mile walk to Clitheroe ended with the party sitting down to rest on any convenient doorsteps, prior to undertaking a walk over the remaining five miles to Stonyhurst.

Quakers

In the mid-17th century fresh ideas about religion were circulating. Men like George Fox, Thomas Jollie and Oliver Heywood opened hearts and minds to a more personal approach. Fox, founder of the Quaker movement, climbed Pendle in 1652 and had his vision of 'a great people' waiting to be gathered. He wrote in his *Journal*:

And the next day we passed on, warning people as we met them of the day of the Lord that was coming upon them. As we went I spied a great high hill called Pendle Hill, and I went on the top of it with much ado, it was so steep; but I was moved of the Lord to go atop of it; and when I came atop of it I saw Lancashire sea; and there atop of the hill I was moved to sound the day of the Lord; and the Lord let me see atop of the hill in what places he had a great people to be gathered …

As he descended the hill, Fox refreshed himself in a spring on the 'roll-over' of the Big End. The spring water was (and remains) deliciously icy. It is one of a multitude of Robin Hood wells. Fox confided:

At night we came to an inn and declared truth to the man of the house, and wrote a paper to the priests and professors, declaring the Day of the Lord, and that Christ was come to teach people himself, by His power and spirit in their hearts … The man of the house spread the paper abroad and was himself mightily affected with the truth. Here the Lord opened to me to see a great people in white raiment by a river side [the River Lune] coming to the Lord.

From the heights of Pendle, Fox would have been able to see the sun glinting on the Irish Sea and (if the weather was very clear) the fell country of North Lancashire and Westmorland where, in coming years, some of his staunchest disciples would be found. Also in view would be Lancaster, with its grim old castle. The founder of Quakerism and many of his supporters were to become familiar with its dark, virtually airless dungeons. Fox spent the 1664-5 winter there, having refused to take the oath in open court. It was during a brush with the law at Derby in 1651 that Fox, who had been charged with blasphemy, bid Justice Bennett quake at the name of the Lord. The worthy justice had retorted by calling him a 'quaker'.

Over a quarter of a century before Fox made his ascent of Pendle Hill, the Ribble Valley had a group which, under the leadership of the Grindleton parson, the Rev. Roger Brierley, impressed many with its simple form of Christian worship. Brierley was summoned to York, probably to be admonished for propounding false doctrines. The first Quakers – yeomen, traders, shepherds, ordinary folk – met in private houses. They found a new, reverent, dignified way of worship, waiting upon God singly, 'as if none was present but the Lord … and so all the rest come, in pure stillness and silence of all flesh and wait'. No one stood between a person and God. Soldiers might break up a meeting, though, so the men sat in a body near the door, with the women and children beyond.

Twiston had many Quakers, among them James Whipp, husbandman, who, refusing to take the oath, was excommunicated and sent to gaol in 1668. Two years later James appeared in court 'for not bringing his wife and child to be buried in the chapell but burying them in the field'. One of the epitaphs in the Quaker burial ground near Twiston, shadowed by Pendle Hill, noted: 'Affliction sore, long time he bore;/Physicians were in vain/Till God did please by death to cease/And ease him of his pain.' Newton became a Quaker meeting place largely through the prayerful activity of William Dewsbury, a shepherd who had been a Cromwellian soldier. When he testified while standing at the market cross in Settle he was thrown down, beaten and left unconscious. So he came into Bowland with his 'message of glad tidings'. The people of Newton gave him an affable reception.

In 1767 John Brabbin of Newton, a retired farmer and cattle dealer, willed £800 and the residue of his personal estate for the teaching of the children of the people called Quakers, 'from wheresoever they come'. His will also allowed for the education of six children of poor persons, not Friends, inhabiting the township of Newton. John Bright, who resided at the school for 18 months, achieved national renown as a politician, popular orator and agitator with Richard Cobden, of Sabden, for the abolition of the Corn Laws. A meeting place for Protestant Dissenters was being used in 1691.

John King, vicar of Chipping from 1622 to 1672, an eventful period spanning the Commonwealth and Restoration of the Monarchy, kept a low profile, changing sides to meet the changes in government. Meanwhile, this prudent man became wealthy through farming. On his death he willed cattle, sheep and agricultural implements to the value of £222 18s. 2½d. Richard Rauthmell, of Whitewell and Grindleton, writing in 1741, observed, 'My two Chapels are in the Alps of the West Riding. I have calculated that I have rid over the alpine mountains to attend and perform Divine Service at Grindleton Chapel above 3,000 miles.'

The Old Faith had its many local adherents, including the Towneleys, Southworths and Shireburns. The Church of England tried to hold its ground against an increasing number of recusants, those who refused to attend Church of England services, many of whom were Catholics. In the 16th century the old lodge at Leagram near Chipping was an illegal meeting place for Catholics. Hidey-holes were provided for the priests in case representatives of the law made a sudden appearance. Edward Arrowsmith, priest, paid the ultimate penalty, death by execution at Lancaster, in 1628.

Nonconformity

Nonconformity had its birth with the passing, in 1662, of the Act of Uniformity. This compelled every clergyman, fellow of a college and schoolmaster to give his 'unfeigned assent and consent' to every statement contained in the Book of Common Prayer. He must also take an oath that resistance to the Crown was sinful and unlawful. Two thousand ministers – over 50 of them in Yorkshire – did not comply, and on St Bartholomew's Day were ejected from their livings. The Act benefited nonconformity by encouraging it to become organised. Two years later, the Conventicle Act forbade, under severe penalties, religious meetings in private homes. The Five-Mile Act drove the non-subscribing ministers into the outlying districts. These two pieces of legislation accentuated the separation of nonconformity from the established church.

Bowland did not have a single 'ejected' parson but its religious life was enriched when it became a place of shelter and refuge for others. Two men who ministered in Bowland and the Ribble Valley, Thomas Jollie (1629-1702) and Oliver Heywood (1630-1702), had been fellow students at Cambridge. Jollie, a member of a family of nonconformist divines and a pupil of Richard Frankland, dissenter, who established the first academy for nonconformist ministers at Rathmell in the Ribble Valley, was imprisoned as a nonconformist. Driven out of his church at Altham in Lancashire, he became an itinerant preacher until he found a settled home at Wymondhouses near Clitheroe. When worshippers gathered in his sitting room, he stood on the second step of a staircase, access to which was by a door that was in two parts. The lower part was kept shut and the upper

78 *St Hubert's Roman Catholic Church, near Dunsop Bridge, was built by the Towneley family.*

part, attached to it by hinges, fell back to form a desk. If informers approached he slipped upstairs, and they could not prove he had been preaching. In more settled times Jollie built a chapel beside his house and ministered there for 40 years. His name is perpetuated through the Jollie Memorial Congregational Church at Barrow.

Oliver Heywood, who had been deprived of the living of Coley, Northowram, represented Presbyterian Dissent. His ministry was nomadic. Notebooks and memoranda have survived to inform us about a man who stood for Independency, that other great branch of nonconformity. It is related that, at the time of the Great Ejectment, he saddled up his horse and left his home and family early one winter day, taking with him neither food nor money. Leaving the reins loose, he let the horse decide which way he went. Heywood found himself outside Monubent Farm, near Bolton-by-Bowland, where the farmer and his family provided food and lodgings. Honest and fearless in his conduct, Heywood became a familiar figure in the Bowland area and parts of adjacent Lancashire, where the 'tingle factor' was provided not just by his preaching but by the distinct chance that the military might intervene as he preached.

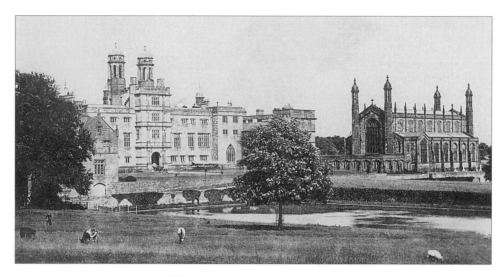

79 *Stonyhurst College, one of the foremost Catholic schools in the land.*

Pasture House, at West Marton, became a regular place of worship and the setting, on 8 July 1678, of the first ordination in Yorkshire by Dissenters. A few years later Heywood reflected, 'I have found my heart more than ordinarily enlarged in pleading for their conversion when amongst them. It is an ignorant place and hath no good preaching in many generations and now there's stirring, who knows what may be done? There are some serious, precious Christians among them with whom I have had sweet communion on Fast Days and the Lord's Supper.' He suffered much, being fined and imprisoned, but remained fully satisfied in his conscience with his 'Non-Conformity', which was the way of God. 'I have so much peace in my spirit that what I do is for the main, according to the word, that if I knew of all the troubles beforehand, and were to begin again, I would persist in this course to my dying day.'

A chapel was built at Horton-in-Craven. In 1816 a larger place of worship was needed. An inscription above the pulpit reads: 'Let no base hireling here intrude/To feed the flock with poisonous food./Kind Shepherd for Thy flock prepare/Pure living streams and pastures fair./Come in ye thirsty, don't delay,/Drink wine and milk, from day to day;/Sweet Jesus calls you come away,/Flee now to Him this very day.' Mount Zion, a solitary building at the roadside near Tosside, is one of the best preserved of the several Independent meeting places. Built in 1812 to serve a scattered farming community, it was attended by between 200 and 300 people who had regularly heard the gospel preached at the home of Miles Thornber, Higher Sandsyke. The Rev. Benjamin Sowden, minister at Horton-in-Craven, laid the foundation stone of the chapel. When he was not invited to become the pastor, 'he fell sick and died after a few days'.

80 *Drawing from an old print of Stonyhurst College.*

The first pastor, the Rev. Hugh Hart, was ordained in 1814. This chapel, with its high, wide pulpit and a stove capable of frying anything up to three yards away, was to change little with the passing years. Tall brown pews, shiny with varnish and much use, have close-fitting doors. In a large enclosure before the pulpit stood a harmonium, which was replaced by an electronic keyboard. Tosside did not lose forever the loneliness of the old forest days. One night in the early 1860s the minister, the Rev. John Robinson, was returning to the manse, part of the church building, after preaching at Settle, when he became conscious of a big black dog following him. As the minister passed along a stretch of road flanked by gloomy woodland, two men sprang out intending to rob him, but the black dog drove them away. The dog spent the night at the manse, leaving next morning, never to be seen again.

Methodism

John Wesley paid several visits to the Bowland area in the mid-18th century. He was especially fond of Chipping, where John Milner, vicar from 1739 to 1777, was a close friend. Milner accompanied Wesley on his travels in England and Scotland. In 1751 the founder of Methodism stayed overnight at the vicarage. The following June he preached in the church on the text 'God was in Christ reconciling the world unto himself', noting in his diary that 'the people were all attention'. A month later Wesley visited Chipping en route for Ireland. A visit in 1753 was marred when noisy men prevented him from preaching in the church. After the service he addressed several parishioners at the vicarage.

When John Wesley and three Inghamite preachers arrived at Roughlee and held a service it was interrupted by a drunken mob from Colne. The leader said

81   *The Independent Chapel at Tosside.*

he was a constable, so Wesley and his friends did not object when they were escorted to Barrowford. Brought before a magistrate, they were told not to preach at Roughlee. Wesley refused. On leaving the court, Wesley and his friends were attacked by the mob and severely beaten. One preacher died shortly afterwards. Even so, several chapels were established in the Pendle area.

Methodist societies like Slaidburn had humble beginnings, the members meeting in cottages. In the mid-19th century, when the population of the area increased rapidly, a chapel was constructed. It served the Methodist cause until its closure in 1999. In January 1766 John Harrison and Sarah Richardson conveyed a piece of ground at Holden Green, near Bolton-by-Bowland, for the residue of a term of 2,000 years from 10 January 1603, without rent, to Henry Walker and six others upon trust. This was 'to permit the piece of ground and the buildings to be erected thereon to be made use of as a chapel or place for performing of public worship and divine service to one or more Protestant or orthodox minister or ministers holding the doctrinal articles of the Church of England required to be subscribed by the minister of any congregation of dissenting Protestants by the Act of William I and Mary'. The chapel was certified as a place of religious worship at the West Riding Quarter Sessions on 12 July 1768.

Before a manse was built, the Holden minister, the Rev. John Gawbeter, lived in rooms under the gallery, drinking water from a stone trough in the hedge bottom some forty yards below the manse. A survivor from the days of farmhouse services was Mill Dam, near Bentham, the home of devout Methodists, where well within living memory people gathered for worship on Sunday afternoons, sitting on forms that at other times were stored in one of the outbuildings. The wooden rostrum was slotted on the back of an ordinary chair set in such a position that the preacher could, if he wished, glance out of the window, which framed a view of Ingleborough.

The village of Rimington was the birthplace of Francis Duckworth, whose hymn tune 'Rimington' achieved world fame by being set to 'Jesus shall reign, where'er the sun'. The hymn, written by Isaac Watts, appealed to those working in foreign missions. Not far from Rimington is the old Methodist chapel of Martin Top. Among the original band of Methodists was one Benjamin Ingham, a Yorkshireman, born in 1712 and admitted to Holy Orders in the Church of England in 1735, who became a missionary in the West Indies. Returning to his native land, he broke with the doctrines of the Methodists – who were still Anglicans – and formed a society called Inghamites. It had a strong following in Bowland, Pendle and West Craven, one of the last remaining chapels being in the village of Salterforth.

Victorian Days

The chapel of Stonyhurst College was built in 1832-5 to a design by J.J. Scoles, a plain miniature copy of the chapel of King's College, Cambridge. Professor Barff decorated the interior in 1854-8. Among the treasures acquired by Stonyhurst was the seventh-century Gospel of St John, a Latin manuscript found in the coffin of St Cuthbert in Durham Cathedral in the year 1105. Elsewhere, a 100-seater Catholic chapel dedicated to St Hubert, the patron saint of hunting, was opened in 1865 on a site beside the road linking Dunsop Bridge and the Trough. For the first eight years the clergy were drawn from Stonyhurst College.

The chapel was a gift of Colonel John Towneley, and the cost was popularly supposed to have been met by part of the winnings when Kettledrum, a Towneley horse trained in the area, won the Epsom Derby of 1861, overtaking the favourite, Dundee, in the final straight. (Kettledrum's last days were spent at the family's stud farm at Dunsop Bridge.) The Towneleys of Thorneyholme were in attendance when the initial sermon was preached by Dr Richard Roskell, Bishop of Nottingham, who returned many times to the area, drawn by a love of angling. On his death the bishop was interred in the churchyard. Mrs Charles Towneley had the church decorated in the 1870s and Mrs John Towneley built a presbytery. When, in 1937, the family estates in the district were sold to the Duchy of Lancaster, the church was excluded.

The Anglican cause at Dalehead was rejuvenated in 1852 when a church was built at Tosside and dedicated to St James. William Wilkinson, of Hellifield, who also endowed it with the sum of £50 annually, derived from his farm at Kettlesbeck, gave the site of the church and parsonage. This William, one of many Williams in the family, died on 10 June 1860. In 1871 Dalehead became a separate ecclesiastical parish, hewn from the huge parish of Slaidburn, and in July 1875 the Wilkinson family presented the church with a large font.

Eight

A Farming Life

In great-grandfather's day, a determined shepherd and his dog who walked from Rathmell in Ribblesdale to the Trough of Bowland, across the moors, traversed the high grazings of seven great sheep farms and did not encounter a single wall or fence. Such a walk, which was unlikely, for each shepherd kept to his own ground, was possible because the various flocks of sheep were 'heafed'. In the absence of man-made boundaries, each kept to its specific area. A lamb drank in a love of locality with its mother's milk. Several generations of one strain of sheep might be seen on the same plot of ground.

Sheep farming on the capacious moors is possible because, in the collie, a farmer has the means of rounding up stock quickly, such as for seasonal jobs or when snow is in the offing. The dog responds to set whistles, which are clear and unemotional. If more than one dog were used, two distinct sets of whistles were needed. The shepherd spent most of his working life on his feet. Full-time shepherds are now rare, the work being done by the farmer using a quad (all-terrain vehicle), with his dog as a pillion passenger until it is required.

Bowland farmers cannot afford to be too clever. Their plans are ruled by the state of the land, by the (somewhat damp) weather and by the slow progress of the seasons in a highland area that acts as a barrier to weather systems racing in from the west. Vast expanses of moorland lie between the well-known valleys. Ling and bilberry deck the dry ridges and peaty hollows are lagged with sphagnum moss. Sheep and grouse are dependent on the heather. Damp spots have abundant insect life, food for grouse chicks.

No food is taken more eagerly by sheep than 'mosscrop', emergent cotton-grass, which appears in early spring. Though commonly known as cotton-grass, the plant is a sedge. The fluffy seed-heads whiten the upland pastures as though with summer snow. Along the edge of the moors is rough pasture-land – tewit-land, to use an old term for the lapwing. In the dales are meadows that yield grass to be stored in barns as winter fodder for the livestock. In modern times, it is taken in a wilted state and wrapped in large plastic bags that do not fit comfortably in barns and are thus stored out-of-doors.

In the settled times of the late 17th and early 18th centuries families with spare cash built for posterity, confident their sons could inherit. Yeoman farmers

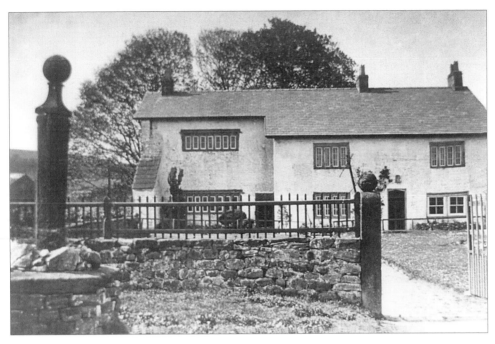

82 *Grange Hall, a notable farm in the upper Hodder Valley, was lost when Stocks reservoir was built.*

joyously vacated homes made of wattle-and-daub and thatch for homes built of stone. Their halls and farms are still a common feature, impressing by their unpretentious use of local materials. Pride of ownership was reflected in ornate doorheads that incorporated the carved initials of husband and wife, with the date. Over the main doorway at Stephen Park, by the upper Hodder, was inscribed the words: 'There is no way for such a guest, Be pleasd to stay for I protest.' Translated, it means: 'There is no thoroughfare and I do object to your going on until you have partaken of our hospitality.' Another carving uncovered during refurbishment work at Stephen Park read, 'He that doth pase must honest be. Not too bold for you see.' Or 'Behave yourself – you're being watched.'

Stephen Park occupies the site of a hunting lodge associated with Hammerton Hall. This farm in latter days was occupied by generations of the Robinson family. Grange Hall, in the same area, where the Cowkings lived, took its name from one of the outlying farms of Kirkstall Abbey. The stables were said to have been a chapel and there was inevitably talk of a secret room, this one being entered by sliding panel. A row of hooks in a space near the chimney was used for smoking beef or mutton. Catlow, at 800ft, was another farm occupied by generations of Robinsons. The house dates from the mid-19th century, with some outbuildings of 17th-century date. When Harrop Hall, near Slaidburn, was re-fronted by the Leigh family in 1719, a stone ball on a plinth was set on either side of the garden gate.

83 *Woman Making Oatcake, from* The Costume of Yorkshire *by George Walker, 1814.*

84 *Yorkshire Farmers, from* Walker's The Costume of Yorkshire.

85 *Yorkshire Horse-dealer, from* Walker's The Costume of Yorkshire.

The Bowland landscape took on a tidier appearance towards the end of the 18th and in the early part of the 19th centuries with the passing of Enclosure Acts. What had been common land was parcelled up, creating a futuristic pattern of boundary walls. It led to significant changes in methods of farming – and re-engaged as hired hands some of the commoners who had lost their livelihoods through the change of use. Acid ground was sweetened when overspread by limestone quarried locally and burnt in field-kilns, the fuel being layers of coal costing about sixpence a hundred-weight. When the kiln had cooled the lime was raked out and carted away to be made into 'lime and earth'. Several tons of the mixture was turned several times as powder and thoroughly blended before being spread on the land.

Bowland's meadows were flower fields, richly coloured by a large variety of blooms. Then came the general transformation, and ploughing and re-seeding with lush types of grass. A visitor to an area such as the Brennand Valley in spring is captivated by the contrast between emerald-green meadows and the rough grazing land on the hills. Here, near the heart of Bowland, is a typical hill farm, with the farmhouse and principal outbuildings standing at an elevation of around 600ft and several thousand sheep being run on an equivalent number of acres of fell-land leased from the water authority. Each of three moorland 'heafs' have a stock of sheep. In the old days, sheep were never brought

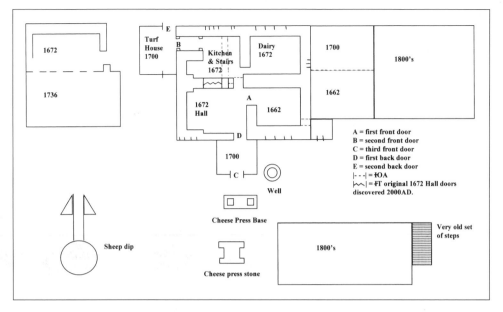

86 *Plan of Stephen Park, a farmstead in the upper Hodder Valley.*

down to the valley for lambing. On the moors are the remains of shepherds' cabins, in which lambing took place. The mortality of lambs was, here and elsewhere, very high. The gruesome story is told of a farmer who, each spring, released an old boar on to the home fell so it might clean up all the dead sheep. The pig lived on carcasses until early summer. A Victorian visitor was shown the remains of a bracken-shed, 'a rough kind of shanty' where bracken or eagle fern, collected during the summer, was stored and was used in winter as bedding for horses and cattle.

Hill Farms

The farms in the upper valley of the Hodder were largely tenanted. Exceptions, before the Great War, were Croasdale and Lamb Hill, which belonged to Col. Hirst, a textile magnate described by a native as 'a sporty chap – what you would call a gentleman'. A hill farmer, in contrast, was small-scale, tough, self-reliant. Norman Swindlehurst was brought up at Brackengarth, one of a string of small farms beside the road leading through Keasden to Bowland Knotts. The farmhouse was of simple construction – stone and slate – the front and back doors being connected by a passage from which the main rooms – living kitchen, sitting-room, back kitchen, dairy – extended. Four bedrooms were available. The mattress was home-made – of calico bought from a travelling draper, stuffed with feathers taken from a goose killed for the Christmas market. The privy was a rose-embowered little edifice situated in the corner of an orchard in which a few damson trees had a struggle to survive.

Most of the ground floor of Brackengarth was covered with blue flagstones of Silurian Age quarried at Helwith Bridge. An exception was the sitting-room, which was boarded. Flagstone was also used for benches (shelves) in the dairy. Norman's mother scrubbed the flags till they shone. When it was going to rain they 'came up damp'. The slopstone (sink) in the back kitchen was of rough sandstone. In the absence of taps, water was collected from a beck with 'ladin' can and bucket'. When it was time for the walls to be limewashed, cob lime was transported from Giggleswick quarry and 'slacked' in a large boiler. The walls were sometimes colour-washed, green or pink.

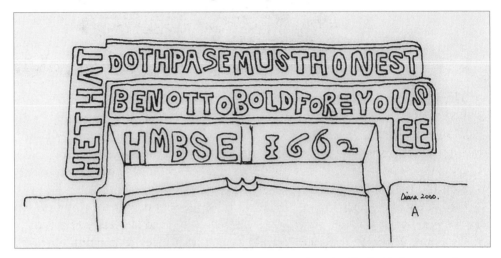

87   *Carving uncovered during refurbishment of Stephen Park. It reads: 'He that doth pase must honest be, Not to bold for you see.' Translated: 'Behave yourself, you're being watched!'*

88   *A second carving uncovered at Stephen Park. It reads; 'There is no way for such a guest, Be pleasd to stay for I protest.' Translated: 'There is no thoroughfare and I object to your going on until you have partaken of our hospitality.'*

89 *Sheep-washing, Keasden.*

The fire, which was never allowed to go out, summer and winter alike, was kindled with paper and heather stalks, then set with peat and sometimes with coal. Once a fortnight, when oatmeal was received from a supplier in Lancaster, via Clapham railway station, mother made riddle-bread on a 'bakstone'. This delicacy was usually stacked in a small basket and eaten overspread with butter. June butter was the best.

Life in remote places bred characters, folk of individual thought and action. The Misses Taylor – Dolly, Grace and Violet – who lived at Hesley Hill, were a case in point. When one of their cows came in season, they waited until nightfall and took it to a neighbour's bull without that neighbour being aware. After dark, they surreptitiously collected cobs of newly-spread lime from a neighbour's field. Hay from their limited acreage of meadowland was transported to the barn in a wheelbarrow. After buying a nine-gallon barrel of beer, they had it delivered to Wham Farm, on the other side of Giggleswick Common, and wheeled it up and over Whelpstone Crag to their home, negotiating several walls en route.

A Bowland hill farmer aimed to be self-reliant. His income was from the sale of surplus livestock. Most of the milk was made into butter, which was sold to the local grocer or swapped for necessary items of food. The Tillotsons of Fair Hill were a large family – mother, father, eight girls and six boys. We know a little about their lives because one of them, born in 1887, talked about the old days and recalled the type of food they ate. Each month a Settle grocer supplied 28 lb of lard, 14 lb of currants and 1 cwt of sugar. On baking day 18 pies and pasties were made; they were consumed over the next two days.

Flour was a vital necessity. The Tillotsons needed 70 lb of flour a week for a baking day, on which there might be ten loaves in the oven at once. Oatmeal was delivered by the sackful so that, once a fortnight, oatcakes might be made. Mrs Tillotson produced 100 oatcakes at a time, each being a yard long. She would dry them on an overhead rack near the fire until crisp; meanwhile they resembled

91   *Sheep-dipping, Catlow Farm, upper Hodder Valley.*

90   *Sheep-washing, Buckmire Farm.*

a wash-leather. Oakcake was eaten with home-produced butter and cheese. The farmer and his family lived largely on pig-meat. During their brief lives the pigs were well fed, receiving generous amounts of oatmeal. The pig-killer slaughtered a pig one day and returned on the next to cut it up, the pieces being suspended from large hooks driven into the ceiling of the kitchen. There were seven hooks to accommodate the two flitches, two hams, two shoulders and some pig-cheek.

The vagaries of the weather tested the mettle of farmfolk. In the terrible spring of 1917, when the Great War was still raging and when families were mourning the loss of local life in France, snow decked the top of Pendle Hill, lingering until well into summer.

92 *Sheep-clipping at Catlow Farm.*

With the ewes short of milk, lambing time was difficult, the calves developing what was described as 'husk' from eating poor quality hay. One March a severe snowstorm was followed by a prolonged hard frost. In April, when lambing began, snow and ice still layered the fields. Sheep could not reach the grass and were fed on what remained of the stock of hay. Milk drawn from the cows was poured into basins and given to the ewes to drink.

Domestic help was cheap. In the 1920s a Bowland farmer went to Lancaster to hire a new girl to work in the house. A shilling was handed over to 'fasten' her. When one girl, having been hired, did not turn up on the appointed day, legal action was threatened. The girl sent the shilling back. Horses did the heavy work at the farm. 'My father had horsitis. We always had about ten or a dozen young horses about us. We'd break 'em in and then sell 'em.' A horse being broken in was fitted with 'breaking-gears' for about a fortnight. 'The bit had flanges. The horse kept chewing them. When a horse had a proper mouth, you could do anything with it.' The tenants of the little hill farms spoke of the few big holdings, such as Lamb Hill and Catlow in the Hodder Valley, with awe.

The 'little men' paid their rent by catching rabbits. An unusual source of income at Slaidburn was making felt hats, mixing rabbit fur with wool from local sheep. The rabbit skins were tacked out on the village green to dry in sunlight and breezes.

93   *Sheep-clipping at Lamb Hill, upper Hodder Valley.*

94   *Women who provided meals when sheep were being clipped at Catlow Farm.*

Sheep

The main income on a hill farm was from sheep, not cattle. The traditional sheep breed was the Lonk, a larger version of the Scotch Blackface, which had a fine quality fleece. The heaf-going instinct that prevented it from roaming was achieved by careful management and by selling off any sheep inclined to wanderlust. Two gimmer lambs, sent from Pendle Hill for wintering to two different places, were reunited on their return to Pendle.

In a bleak area, a ewe might not have nourishment for two lambs, so goats were kept. They dropped their kids early in the year and a good milk flow occurred at the time the sheep were lambing. At Catlow, the billy and five goats summered on the fell, using a crude shelter provided by the farmer.

Clipping time at a farm with over 1,000 sheep involved neighbours and friends and was known as a 'boon clip',

95   *Goose-plucking time, Keasden.*

a custom that survived until the 1950s. Then the erstwhile helpers were keen to use the limited summer sunshine in haymaking. A fortnight before sheep were clipped the local beck was 'demmed' and the fleeces were washed, a process that removed the last traces of the salve that had been applied to the skins on the previous November. As the tainted water flowed down the beck, trout were stupified and could easily be caught. 'Folk worked – and got fed. It was just a big happy party.'

Men clipped on stocks (wooden forms). George Wallbank recalled the boon clip at Catlow:

> As soon as the men arrived, they entered the house, donned their overalls and had something to eat – mostly sandwiches and cakes. There wasn't a mad rush. Now time's money. When I was a lad, the men were smoking their pipes and chewing black twist. They'd clip a sheep or two and have a talk. Ted Robinson kept 'em in order. He also used to catch sheep for t'clippers. I've seen Ted bring two sheep, one under each arm.

When a sheep was 'let off t'stock' it was collected by Bill Tillotson, who marked it with the identification marks lost when the fleece was removed.

96   *Sign at a farm near Leagram Hall. 'Laund' was an old name for a deer-park.*

97   *A tup of the Swaledale breed of sheep.*

Tea in buckets and sandwiches fortified the thirty or so clippers and catchers during the day. 'We clipped away. There'd be joke-telling and leg-pulling. When we finished, about seven o'clock, then we'd all go and have a wash. Dishes of water were arranged on a wall-top for the men to use. Then there'd be more to eat.' If anyone had a reserve of energy, they might dance in the emptied barn to music provided by fiddle or accordion. The floor was not especially smooth but as the men wore big boots it didn't matter so much. Non-dancers sat on bales of hay. The dance continued until daybreak. In the 1930s four Dalehead men who were 'nifty clippers' travelled to Bradford and snipped the fleeces from a group of sheep at the start of a process – devised for publicity purposes – during which a suit would be made within 24 hours, from sheep's back to man's back.

98   *Clitheroe farmers with 'Thorndale Lady Bates'.*

99 *Tom Varley,
drystone-waller,
who lived at Todber,
near Gisburn.*

Farmers were quick to spot ailments in their stock. Some men were widely known as specialists. One of them was skilled at attending to 'sturdy', a complaint that led to a parasite being lodged in the sheep's skull. It was caused by a tapeworm picked up from the droppings of a stray dog, or from rabbits if they were numerous. A sheep with sturdy 'went round in a circle, ten or a dozen yards for a start and eventually following its tail'. The specialist located a point where the skull was 'as soft as putty, about the size of half a crown', and drove a hole into it, recovering 'a bladder full of water and seeds'. When it had been removed, invariably with the quill from a goose, the wound was dressed using salve, even tar.

Raising sheep on hill farms, such as at Dalehead, was 'a lot of hard work for nothing' during the depression years between the wars. Vic Robinson, who was reared at Stephen Park, recalled when spare lambs were driven for sale to Copy Nook, near Bolton-by-Bowland. Once, when the price was a mere 11s. each, the lambs were driven back to the farm. Subsequently, at Slaidburn, they were sold when the bid reached 15s.

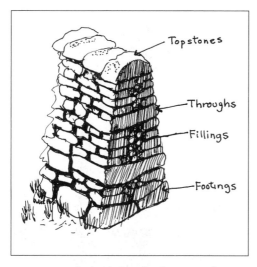

100   *Sectional view of a drystone wall.*

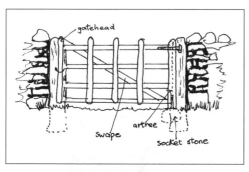

101   *Gate in a drystone wall.*

Cattle

As related, cattle rather than sheep feature in the medieval history of Bowland and Pendle. At the edge of living memory, when many hill farms were tenanted, there might be no more than 30 acres of 'inland' and around 16 head of cattle. Herds were small, self-contained. A farmer aimed to sell three or four cows a year – enough to 'pay t'rent, wi' a bit left ower'. At the turn of the 19th century, cattle were milked by hand, twice a day, in tiny shippons flavoured by the scents of hay and dung. None of the milk left the little hill farms as milk. The cream was separated and kept until churning day, when most of it was transformed into butter. The separation process took place using a 'lead', a shallow metal tray with tapered sides to which cream clung; the remaining 'blue' milk was drained away.

The rumble of an end-to-end churn was a familiar sound in the farm kitchen. Churning was a tedious job, especially in summer when the cream was slow to turn. If a 'round pound' of butter were made, its origin was noted by the use of a distinctive wooden stamp, made of sycamore, which did not taint the butter. Or it was patted into blocks with 'Scotch Hands', wooden bats, one side of each being ridged. Surplus butter from Dalehead was usually retailed in the industrial areas of East Lancashire, notably Colne and Nelson.

Peat

June was the month for cutting peat with a special winged spade and rearing the turves into conical heaps. The drying process continued until, in good weather, the peats could be carted to the farms. Some were stored in peat-houses; others were formed into stacks at the gable ends of the farmhouses. A peat fire rarely went out, the glow from yesterday's fire remaining when the 'first down' in the morning attended to it. The Tillotsons of Fair Hill did not use a cob of coal for 30 years. Each summer they recovered 80 cart loads of peat from the moor. Peat was cut from the blanket bog on Pendle. Robert Hargraves, of Wilkinson's Farm, Barley, remembered visiting the hill with his aunt, who helped to turn the turves so that they would dry in sun and breeze. The men, in a time-sharing rotation of work, cut enough peat for a load and then transported back to the farm any peat that was dry.

Haymaking

The blacksmith's life was hectic in the run-up to haytime. He repaired the wooden frame known as 'shelving' that fitted on a cart to increase its holding capacity, and attended to the sleds that, drawn by horses, were used on steep ground. At one hill farm, haytime was said to begin when Dad threw the wooden rakes into a water-trough to make the wood swell, ensuring that the teeth would not drop out. Irish labourers, known as July Barbers, were employed for haytime for as little as £6 a month, board and lodging provided. Their services were needed when getting the hay was basically a hand operation, with no strawing (strewing-out) or side-delivery machines. Many of the Irishmen lived in Mayo, in the west of Ireland, being hired for haytime work at Bentham in late June.

Meadows were mown by hand. A team of men with scythes worked in unison using long-bladed, straight-shafted scythes. A good scythesman cut a swathe from five to six feet wide. He rose from his bed as early as 4 a.m., breakfasting on porridge, whey and fatcakes. At lunchtime, hung-beef and potatoes was served. The beef had been

102 *Tom Leedham, a breeder of fine collies, who became English shepherd champion in the 1960s.*

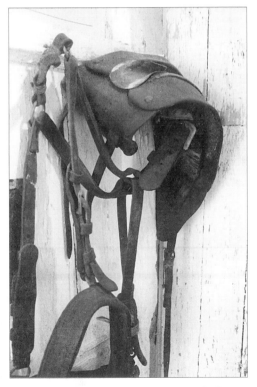

103 *Horse harness on display at the Slaidburn Heritage Centre.*

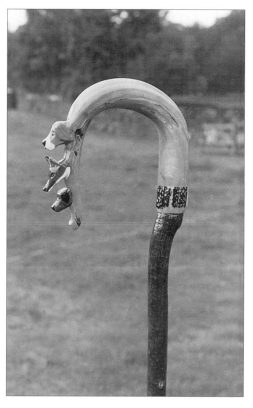

cut into strips and dried. It was reconstituted before being cooked. A hayfield meal was known as the 'baggin'.

In late Victorian times the Barley side of Pendle held many small-holdings, let for £3 an acre and noted for the quality of their herbage. Hayseed was swept from the floors of the barns during the winter to be sold to farmers who were ploughing during the following spring. At haytime, the shepherd employed by the small-holders sat on top of the hill within sight of the haymakers. If a storm cloud blew up from the direction of Blackpool he waved a black flag. The hay was 'piked' into a weatherproof heap in case the storm broke. At the 'back o' Pendle' farmers consulted an unusual sundial. When the evening shadow creeping down the hillside reached a spot where two walls came to a point it was five o'clock, time for tea!

104 *Head of a shepherd's crook, fashioned from the horn of a tup.*

105 *Colley Holme, one of the old farms of the upper Hodder Valley.*

106   *Remains of a cast-iron fireplace in a ruined Bowland farm.*

107   *Conical heaps of peat, drying in sunshine and wind.*

108   *Haymaking at Brackengarth, Keasden.*

109   *Haymaking, upper Hodder Valley.*

110   *A Land Car made from a stripped-down saloon car.*

Mechanisation

An advance on horse-drawn machinery
was the adaptation of old cars, Model
T Fords and Austin 12s, as mowing
machines. Rufus Carr, whose family
moved to Rimington in 1926, is
remembered as a man who frequented
scrapyards in Lancashire, bought up
old cars for as little as 17s. 6d. and
converted them into motor-mowers,
each being chain-driven from the back
axle. Rufus charged £17 for such an
appliance, expecting it to last at least
ten years. In one year he bought over

111   *The Hannam family in the upper Hodder
pose with a motorcycle.*

50 old cars from a scrap merchant. The Austin 12 was a favourite for stripping
down, being heavy, with a four-cylinder petrol engine.

Ever-inventive, Rufus put two gear boxes in an old Austin 12 so that it
might be used as a small-time tractor, useful for all manner of farm jobs, including
muck-spreading. He attached a plough to one vehicle at the request of a customer.
The efficiency was increased when two tyres were put to each of the back
wheels, the normal tyre and another that fitted over it. The wire rim of the
additional tyre was cut off and slots were made to improve the gripping.

Nine

SPORTING DAYS

Early in the 17th century, Nicholas Assheton of Downham had the means and leisure to live a sporting life. Moreover, he kept a detailed record of what he had seen, slain and consumed. Nicholas went fox-hunting on Harrop Fell. He ate the 'chine and the liver' of a stag shot by Ralph Anderson. In early September, joining a hunt 'into Bolland', Nicholas saw a stag killed at Harden and another a little above Harden. It was 'excellent sport' he wrote in his journal, adding, 'So to Whalley and supped.' That same month he visited Burnside and Whitendale, which were 'overrun with good deer'. As 18th-century landowners beautified their estates, the lowlands of Bowland took on a well-wooded appearance. Beech (*Fagus sylvatica*) and ash (*Fraxinus excelsior*) were popular. The sycamore (*Acer pseudoplatanus*), now common, was introduced from the continent in the 15th century.

The Victorian gentry lived better than any English upper class had done before them. Life on their estates was sustained by an enormous reservoir of cheap labour. The Peel family of Knowlmere organised dinner parties on a grand scale. One of them was attended by the merry widow of Henry Wigglesworth (a parson who died in 1838). She was well dressed, her outfit including a Paris bonnet and some high-heeled shoes that had been collected by her during a recent visit to France. This lady, unperturbed by primitive transport, travelled to grand balls held in York in what was known as her 'yellow chariot'. The old Bowland squirearchy, augmented by the 'new-rich' of the Industrial Revolution and untroubled by the taxman, maintained their social standing through the ownership of land and their commitment to a sporting life. They hunted foxes and deer and shot both red and black grouse, pheasant, partridge and hare. Knowlmere, under Judge Peel, had a relatively small grouse moor but abundant copses and fields for the rearing and eventual slaying of pheasant and partridge.

The heyday of the big Bowland estates was the Edwardian Sunset, before the Great War shattered the social structure. The gamekeeper ruled life on the moors to the extent that a farmer with sheep-grazing rights had to have the head keeper's agreement before visiting the moor to inspect or gather his sheep. Gamekeepers ensured that natural predators like crows and foxes did not trouble the chosen species. They routinely shot any birds that had hooked

112 *Anglers by the Calder, Whalley. From Whitaker's* History of Whalley.

beaks. In 1828, at Browsholme, a notice relating to the preservation of game was issued under the authority of the Duke of Buccleuch. Tenants should give every assistance to the Keeper and Bowbearer of the Forest of Bowland 'and are hereby requested to warn off and discharge every person that may come onto their separate farms without the written leave of His Grace or the Bowbearer'.

Conifer plantations appeared on many estates. An Asiatic flavour was imparted through the planting of groves of rhododendron as cover for pheasants, the ancestors of which had been jungle fowl. In due course, at Gisburn, a strange deer was imported for sport. It was the sika, which had evolved on the Japanese archipelago and arrived in Bowland via Woburn and Powerscourt, just south of Dublin. Inevitably, the sika spread through Bowland. The high-pitched squeals of the stag announcing its presence to the hinds during the rut sounded from a distance like the whistling of a north-country Pan.

Grouse Shooting

The Rev. William Assheton, one of the old-style shooters of grouse, had a fowling piece of great age. When he saw a line of beaters appear on the skyline, he would shout, 'The French are coming! The French are coming!' At their best, the moors had a well-balanced stock of grouse and sheep and the heather was kept young by 'swiddening' (burning in strips). The size of the grouse population is indicated

113 Moorcock Inn, *Waddington Fell,*
featuring a grouse, prime quarry in Bowland.

by the experience of the eight guns who, in 1915, visited Tarnbrook Fell. They brought down 2,929 birds. On the following day 1,763 birds were shot; and on the next day, with two added guns, the bag was 1,279, making 5,971 birds for three consecutive days. Before the end of October these moors had yielded 15,176 birds.

Around 1900, Jules Hirst, 'half Hungarian', a wealthy cotton manufacturer with a house in Scotland, had the shooting rights over most of the Hodder basin. During the shooting season the family rented Town Head at Slaidburn (a custom that continued until the late 1930s). The Hirsts owned Lamb Hill, one of two big sheep farms at the head of the Hodder valley, where there was extensive moorland. Colonel Hirst, son of Jules, who succeeded his father, presided over Coats' Cotton in Glasgow (and also had a mill in Skipton). The Colonel had a Rolls Royce and a Mercedes, which he used for transporting shooters and essential supplies to the selected moor. The farmer at Lamb Hill supplied one sheep a week during the season, taken to Town Head by one of the chauffeurs to help feed the large staff.

Elsewhere, rough shooting was practised. At Bowland Knotts a visiting sportsman shot any number of hares and handed them over to a beater who would carry them. The hapless man already had a large bag of cartridges on his back and a spare gun on the crook of the arm. For a day's attendance he was paid 10s. Grouse-shooters walked to the butts: 'We walked up, we walked down; we went home and next morning we walked up to the moor again.' Nowadays the shooters are transported on good tracks in Land Rovers. The gamekeeper's role has changed in modern times; he has become a guardian of the moors. Generally the number of grouse has declined – victims of disease, over-grazing by sheep and, perhaps, climate change.

The Duke of Westminster owns the Abbeystead Estate, which includes about 16,000 acres of moorland. He is a key member of the Moorland Association, one of its aims being to halt the loss of heather by adopting good moorland management, and has kept up a satisfactory population of grouse. The Duke has also launched the Bowland Foods Company, which is dedicated to marketing meat products from this area, initially beef and lamb but in due course other products such as grouse. The Duke's keepers occasionally conduct interested members of the public to the moors by tractor and trailer and, amid the heather, and with the crowing of grouse to be heard, talk about a year in the life of a moorland keeper.

On Tarnbrook Fell are the copious droppings from a mixed colony of lesser black-backed and herring gulls. During the nesting season they produce a sustained, concerted wailing. With regard to other moorland species, Bowland is the most successful area in England for breeding hen harriers. In the nesting season of 1980, a census recorded that 39 female hen harriers were incubating eggs. Other moorland nesters are meadow pipit, curlew and, of course, grouse. On lower slopes and in-bye land nest good numbers of lapwing, redshank and snipe.

Fishing

The Peels of Knowlmere, near Dunsop Bridge, created what was probably the first fish hatchery in England. The Ribble, being spring-fed from limestone, is rich in natural food for fish of all ages. Salmon still make spawning runs to gravel beds at the headwaters, assisted at several industrial weirs by 'salmon ladders', each a series of pools extending from tailwater to headwater. Salmon use gravel beds in the upper Hodder and some of its tributaries. Dalehead, which

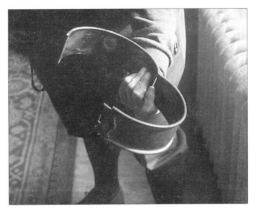

114 *A collar designed for a buckhound is preserved at Browsholme Hall.*

115 *St Hubert, patron saint of hunters, as portrayed in stained glass at the Catholic church near Dunsop Bridge.*

had an impressive spring run of salmon, was no longer available to migratory fish when Stocks reservoir was constructed. Until that time, the Hodder was considered by many anglers to be the finest sea trout river in England. The river is inclined to be acidic and so the trout are relatively small; they grew more slowly than the Ribble fish, were noticeably deeper in the shoulder, and tended to spawn in December, somewhat later than fish at the gravel-beds of the Ribble.

For centuries, before conservation measures were introduced, salmon and sea trout were netted at many points in the estuary. The abbeys of Whalley and Sallay (Sawley) had estuarial fishing rights. In 1300, when there was considerable over-fishing, Sawley lamented that 'fish in the Ribble now rarely come up to Sawley because of the Whalley monks and are dearer when they do come by a third of a penny'. When the Dissolution put the fishing into private hands, netting continued to be the main means of catching migratory fish. The netting season began in February, so there must have been a good run of spring fish. A 16th-century document associated with the Farington family made a distinction between salmon, forktails (grilse) and mort (sea trout). In 1863 many more salmon than usual were spawning in the Ribble, the Hodder and Croasdale Beck at Slaidburn. The improvement was ascribed to the introduction of a new close season and the enforced introduction of nets with a larger mesh.

Three years later fishing was regulated by a Board of Conservators. They were funded by the sale of licenses for net and rod and by fines imposed for infringements. The river Calder was becoming polluted by industry but Ribble and Hodder still ran clear and cool. In 1871 an impressive 10,142 salmon were netted and 302 licensed rods (each licence costing 10s.) accounted for 202 salmon. Of these, only 26 were caught in the Hodder. An exultant Ware & Ware, fishmongers and game-dealers at Preston, took out a newspaper advertisement, including a poem that began 'Ribble Salmon! Ribble Salmon!/Choicest of the finny tribe./Fresh and sparkling from the river,/Caught with morning's flowing tide.'

Netting was still intense at the close of the 19th century. The Towneley Estates operated between Thornyholme and Swannyholme and, later, from Knowlemere to below Doeford Bridge. Stonyhurst netted the pools from above this bridge to Ribchester. Overkill at the turn of the century led to riparian owners and the Fishery Board taking a first, voluntary step to abolish netting. 'Lesser men', nonetheless, continued with it, slyly. In some years there were large spring 'runs' of lampreys, which also dug redds in the gravel beds for their eggs. Crayfish were reported from the upper reaches. Poaching salmon in the upper Hodder was rife until a transformation of the valley wrought by the dam built by Fylde Water Board. One of the Cowking family, of Grange Hall, a fine building demolished by the reservoir-makers, had a rough-haired collie called Tidy which grabbed passing salmon and brought them to the river bank. Another farmer, who was muck-spreading during a salmon run, used his fork to spear a fish that

116 *Red hinds and a calf. Deer were emparked and released for hunting on specified days.*

made the scales dip at 32 lb. Everyone called to see the monster salmon except the beck-watcher, who had been lured into the *Hark to Bounty* at Slaidburn and rendered 'market fresh'.

Local people could scarcely cope with the weight of salmon taken surreptitiously from the river. Steaks were boiled or fried. What could not be eaten was mashed up and served to the hens. The poacher's technique was first to lure the bailiff away so 'tha knew where tha'd got him'. One man excused his behaviour by saying, 'I got a bit o' satisfaction out of doing summat I'd every right to do – but which t'law of t'land said I mustn't do.' He was very satisfied on the night he lifted 70 'nice fish' from the water. Poachers enticed the salmon towards the gaff at night by shining a light on the water. The Rev. T. W. Castle, new to the parish, denounced from the pulpit the widespread poaching of fish. On the following morning, as he prepared to leave the Vicarage, he found a prime salmon hanging from the door-sneck. He did not subsequently preach about poaching.

Fly-fishermen tempted salmon (which do not feed while on a spawning run) with such lures as 'plain turkey wing fly'. Those seeking trout had a wide choice of flies, including black gnat, drake black, woodcock black, March brown, snipe

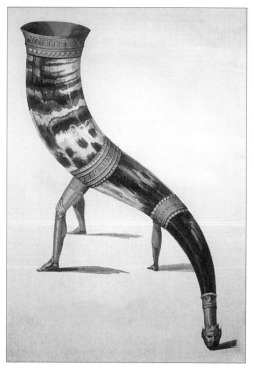

117　*An old horn owned by Lord Ribblesdale, from Whitaker's* History of Craven.

grey, dun bloe, moorgame brown and the curiously-named cock-a-bonddu. Thos Johnson, the writer of an informative guide book, considered these were at their best under cloud and with a southerly wind. Other species of fish in the Ribble towards the end of the 19th century, when Thos Johnson's pen was most active, were trout, chub, dace, gudgeon and eels.

Hunting

Captain Peter Ormerod of Wyresdale Park was joint master with Lord Ribblesdale of the Ribblesdale Buck-hounds, which at one time was kennelled at Gisburn Mill. The Hunt pursued black fallow, which were penned in a large enclosure beside Skirden Brook, Bolton-by-Bowland, and were in charge of a deer-keeper called Draper. Prior to a hunt, selected deer would be carted in a horse-drawn trailer into the countryside and set free.

The fallow deer were extirpated (to use an ancient term) and replaced by the aforementioned sika deer, which were originally kept in captivity until needed for hunting. Inevitably some escaped, and eventually a sizeable population – some 200 animals – built up. Numbers are now kept down through selective culling by stalkers associated with the Bowland Deer Preservation Society. An effort to maintain the social grouping is not helped by poachers who visit farmlands in the early hours and shoot deer (crossbows are favoured) when the animals are illuminated by powerful lights.

Ten

INDUSTRY

Mining

Bowland and Pendle were ransacked for minerals by generations of miners who were known collectively as 't'owd man'. Spoil heaps hold traces of both pink and white barite (barium sulphate), quartz, fluorspar, galena (lead ore) and calomine (zinc ore). About the year 1600, Sir Bevis Bulmer recruited workmen from the south and gentlemen from London and 'got good stores of Silver Ore' from a mine near the junction of Brennand and Whitendale. The veins proved too variable for continuous development. When the London gentlemen returned to the mines in 1655, silver proved elusive. John Webster noted in *Metallographia* (1671), that they were men 'neither of free Purses to follow such a Work, nor of skill or government fit to manage such an Enterprise'.

The mines were re-opened briefly in the 18th century by the Clitheroe Mining Company, who were seeking lead. Beside the road from Dunsop Bridge to the

118   *Clitheroe's main street in 1921.*

Trough, and at the foot of Smelt Mill Clough, is a dwelling on an old foundation known as Smelt Mill Cottages. It is almost certainly the site of the smelt mill dealing with galena from the Sykes and Brennand mines. The Brennand veins were intercepted by way of bell-pits, shafts and a day level driven in from the foot of the hill. The lead ore was transported over the hill to the smelt mill on pack animals.

More famous as a silver mine than Brennand was Skelhorn, on the Yorkshire side of Ings Beck, to the north of Pendle Hill and a mile south of the village of Rimington. The larger of two veins was worked for barytes; the other yielded a goodly amount of galena. The surface ores of Skelhorn were, like those at Brennand, noted for the high content of silver. This raised the matter of how the mine should be classified. Any working that yielded gold or silver sufficient to pay the cost of smelting and working the same qualified for being a Mine Royal and had to be declared. Rather than forfeiting an especially rich mine, an owner might 'conceal' it and work it illegally. Another way to avoid forfeiture, was to mix the silver-rich ore with poor stuff from neighbouring veins. The two might then be smelted as an ore of low enough value to avoid the involvement of the Crown.

The historian John Webster was fascinated by stories told of William Pudsay (1556-1629). Webster described him as 'an ancient esquire and owner of Bolton Hall juxta Bolland', who achieved celebrity as a counterfeiter. In the reign of Queen Elizabeth – who was said to be his godmother – Pudsay 'did there get good store of Silver Ore and converted it to his own use (or rather coined it as many believe, there being many florins marked with an Escalope, which the people of that Country call Pudsay's Shillings to this day)'. The escalope mark (scallop shell) was that of the Mint at the Tower of London for the years 1584 to 1586. Webster tried to obtain a specimen of Pudsay's handiwork, without success. It is unlikely that Pudsay Shillings existed as such. There is no record of counterfeiting. The charge for which William sought pardon was that of concealing a Royal Mine. Arthur Raistrick, a historian of recent date, wrote, 'It seems more likely that the shillings were medallions or tokens made for distribution among Pudsay's friends.'

Pudsay is said to have been debt-ridden. He consulted two elves, Lob and Michil, who directed him to a mine (Skelhorn) on Bolton property, where he would find a vein of silver. He took their advice and minted his own shillings to pay his debts. When news reached the authorities, soldiers were sent to apprehend him. The elves provided him with a silver bridle, on wearing which his horse would never tire. He rode off, leapt into the river from the rim of a sheer 90ft-high cliff that became known as Pudsay's Leap, and made for London, where he obtained the Queen's pardon. The meeting with the Queen is said to have occurred aboard the royal barge on the Thames. He promised not to repeat his illegal activities and, in 1668, is said to have mortgaged the Skellhorn mine for £3,500; it was never redeemed.

119   *Slaidburn Silver Band on the green, 1890s.*

This fanciful story, for which there are variants, sprang largely from the imagination of H.A. Littledale, who owned the Bolton estate in the middle of the 19th century. It was doubtless Littledale who introduced the silver bridle and the friendly hobgoblins he named Lob and Michil. The 'magic' bridle was being used in other contemporary stories, a local example being that of Nick Nevison, the highwayman who fled from gentlemen of the law following the intervention of a spirit guarding the Ebbing and Flowing Well, which lies at the base of Giggleswick Scar. (The law caught him, however, and he was hanged at York in 1684.)

Pudsay's crime was in operating a silver mine without royal warrant. It has been suggested that Pudsay Shilling was the name given to such coins which, instituted by Queen Elizabeth, were introduced into the north by one of the Pudsay family put in charge of the new coinage. Lob and Michil, the hobgoblins, featured in local Mischief Night celebrations which originated in the pagan custom of sun worship and occurred on 30 April.

Quarrying

Sandstone quarried on Waddington Fell and Longridge Fell was a primary source of building material over a wide area. It was also shaped into millstones, the coarse nature of the material ensuring that grain did not overheat during milling. (From such use came the geological term, Millstone Grit.) Most of the houses at Slaidburn dating from the 18th and 19th centuries were made of sandstone quarried on Waddington Fell, which was also a prime source of sandstone flags for roofing purposes.

120   *Funeral of George Booth at Clitheroe.*

The Ribble Valley limestone quarrying tradition stretches back over four centuries to the days when lime was burnt for domestic use or to sweeten sour land. Visitors to limestone areas find long disused field kilns. Before the rail link between Clitheroe and Blackburn was established in 1848, pack animals known as lime-gals, operating in trains of from 10 to 20 animals, conveyed lime to Burnley and returned with loads of coal. Each animal was capable of carrying 200 lb of lime or coal.

At the Bold Venture Limeworks near Clitheroe, in 1848, the owner posted a notice with the object of encouraging habits of sobriety and temperance. He also wished to promote the comfort and happiness of the several persons employed at the works and their families. His idea was to give a gratuity of one week's wages to every man and boy who 'shall be in my service on the 1st of November, 1849, either as Book-keeper, Quarryman, Lime-burner, Drawer, Carter, Labourer or in any other capacity and who shall make a solemn Declaration before a Magistrate that he has not … partaken of any spirituous Liquor, Ale, Beer or other intoxicating drink.'

Before the century ended, cement-making had arrived on a commercial scale. Cement is made by heating limestone with small amounts of other materials, such as clay or shale, in a rotary kiln to a temperature of 1,450°C. In the process, the stone chemically changes into a hard substance resembling volcanic rock known as clinker. This is then ground with a little gypsum to form ordinary Portland cement. In 1936 the Ribblesdale Cement Company acquired the company

121 *Patients at St John's Military Hospital, Clitheroe.*

and steady expansion, from six kilns, raised the annual production in the 1970s to 800,000 tonnes. Ribblesdale Cement's two parent companies merged under the ownership of RTZ, and subsequently the company was renamed Castle Cement. In 1983 a sum of £30 million was invested in a new dry-process kiln. This continues to operate in tandem with two older wet-process kilns to produce about 1.3 million tonnes a year. Ribblesdale is one of the three cement works in the UK arm of Heidelberger Zement, which is Europe's largest cement producer.

Textiles

John Brabin, a dyer and cloth dealer at Chipping in the 17th century, distributed weft and yarn to the local handloom weavers and received in return the woven cloth, which he then dyed. A kindly man, he left money for the establishment of a village school. The market town of Longridge developed around a 15th-century chapel and expanded considerably in the 18th century when handloom weaving throve and sandstone quarries were opened on Tootle Heights. A Mr Boothman, born in 1841 at Newby, near Rimington, was fond of recalling when his family wove cotton cloth on handlooms. The cloth was marketed at Colne and Nelson. Weavers with cloth on their backs walked to the towns, and on handing over their products were given further orders from agents.

Mr Boothman was a bobbin-winder at the age of seven. Then, as a handloom weaver, he supplemented the family income in a mill at Howgill where what were known as alpacas, checks and plains were produced. He recalled when

122   *Victorian estate workers, members of the Parkinson family, at Bolton-by-Bowland.*

123   *Clarion House, on the southern flank of Pendle Hill, was much used by walkers and cyclists.*

power-loom weaving was introduced to the area. It was a turbulent time for hand craftsmen, who were thrown out of work and marched as a mob through the Aire Valley. In their fury they drew plugs from boilers, stopping work at the hated mills. The population of Grindleton, which in 1821 numbered 1,125, was half that number by 1870 as a consequence of families moving out of the parish to work in the mills.

Around 1770 four spinners had to be recruited to produce yarn required by a single weaver in a West Riding town. The help of rural workers was recruited by such families as the Akroyds of Halifax, who sent combed wool to Tosside, Wigglesworth, Dunsop Bridge and Austwick for spinning at farmhouses and cottages. Some of the milestones set up in Bowland indicated the distance to Halifax. Packhorse transport was expensive. It cost half a crown to move a pack of wool from Halifax to Dunsop Bridge. Messages and money for the agents were wrapped up in the wool as a precaution against robbers and vagabonds.

The census of 1801 showed that two-thirds of Lancastrians lived in the country; 50 years later two-thirds were townies. The village of Downham, on the

124   *Smelt Mill Cottages, between Sykes and Dunsop Bridge.*

125   *Domestic spinning, from* The Costume of Yorkshire, *1814.*

coalless side of Pendle, is smaller and less busy than it was when handloom weaving was in vogue and the clack-and-shutter of looms might be heard from old houses with long windows designed as weaving sheds. Half the income of a family would come from weaving and the rest from farming. With industrialisation, many migrated 'over Pendle Hill' to the burgeoning cotton towns.

At Newchurch-in-Pendle in 1826 the population totalled 769 and there were 387 handlooms. Thos Johnson wrote in 1884 of the threat posed to the life of Whalley by 'the principle of manufactures, aided by the discoveries lately made in the two dangerous sciences of Chemistry and Mechanics'. There were undoubtedly benefits. 'At the same time we must all have been too often painfully struck with the devastation that "the principle of manufactures" has committed on many of the venerable and picturesque spots in this district.'

Traditionally an agricultural community, in 1801 Chipping had 827 inhabitants, most of whom worked on the land. By 1831, through industrialisation, the population had risen to 1,334. Chipping Brook provided the power for cotton spinning, one among eight industries dependent on water power. Grove Row, built as a workhouse for the poor in 1824, was used for this purpose until 1840, when it accommodated millworkers. So many people arrived for mill work that a street of congested houses was nicknamed Rat Row. In 1851 a local trade directory gave cotton spinning and the manufacture of spindles and flys as the most important trades.

Kirk Mill, with a valley site just outside the village, was referred to in *History and Topography of Chipping* in 1843 as a factory that presented a model of order and cleanliness:

> Ordinarily, it is worked by a breast-wheel thirty two feet in diameter, supplied with water from an extensive reservoir, contiguous to the premises; but there is also an effective steam engine on the spot, which is occasionally used to supply the water, after a continuance of drought. The mill is lighted with gas throughout, for the supply of which there is a complete and elegant apparatus, adjoining the works. This is a truly admirable arrangement, and one so rare, on that scale, as to be considered almost a curiosity.

126 *Factory children, from* The Costume of Yorkshire.

At the start of the slump in the cotton trade in 1862, mill-owners at Low Moor, Clitheroe issued over 1,000 pints of free soup to their employees each week. By 1909 Roughlee Mill had become a laundry. Soon afterwards a boating lake and pleasure gardens were developed. Samuel Smalley, who was born at Sawley in 1879, was taught the craft of clog-block cutting and became the last practitioner of a once-busy occupation. Clogs were commonly

127   *Narrowgates Mill, Barley,* c.*1920.*

128   *Mr Turner of Slaidburn, with clog soles cut and stacked to dry.*

129   *George Robinson, repairing clogs at Catlow Farm.*

worn in the textile towns, being sturdy enough to stand rough wear and tear on the stone setts and enabling a worker at the loom to stand proud of the damp floors of weaving sheds. At the time when Samuel married, he had received 8d. a dozen for men's size blocks, 7d. a dozen for the women's size and 4d. a dozen for blocks suitable for children's clogs. His brother, Luke Smalley, supplied the alder wood.

Lancashire mill workers, having saved a little money during the winter, spent some of it on Saturday afternoons in summer visiting Bowland on horse-drawn vehicles. Bolton-by-Bowland was a popular venue. The aptly-named *Coach and Horses*, kept by a tenant farmer and his wife, provided meals of salmon, roast duck, chicken, eggs and cream. Mr Wright, who owned Bolton Hall, allowed his gardens and stables to be inspected by the visitors. It was recalled that the saddle room walls were covered by shining harness, rows of whips and coaching horns. In the middle of the largest room were the three skeletons – one of a horse, another of a man – said to be a Frenchman – and a hound. There was also a coach and four which, when taken on roads where the boughs of trees hung low, required two footmen at the back constantly to call 'heads'. Heads were promptly ducked.

Eleven

COMMUNICATIONS

Roads

In 1926 Father Wright, the Procurator of Stonyhurst, employed John L. McAdam in the construction of the road from the new Hodder Bridge to Hurst Green, and was thus among the first to recognise the advantages of the macadamised surface. Elsewhere roads were waterbound, dusty in summer, puddly in winter. John Watson, staying overnight at a Slaidburn inn during the 19th century, scratched on a window: 'Oh, Bowland, thy roads are infamous,/Thy people's manners worse,/To live among thy hills/Is a most grievous curse.'

A stage-coach was operating locally by 1640. Edward Parker, writing to his father at Browsholme Hall in 1663, noted: 'my journey in no ways pleasant, being forced to ride in the boote all the waye … This travel hath so indisposed me yt I am resolved never to ride againe in ye coaches.' Bowland was at the back of beyond. Richard Rauthmell, a Bowland parson, informed a London colleague in 1741, 'Your letter directed to the curate of Grindleton by Bradford Bagg lay several weeks upon the Road.' There was no regular communication between Bradford and Bowland either by Post or Carrier. 'All letters from London to this Country are sent by Preston in Lancashire Bagg.'

In the 1790s, when William Tipping borrowed money from his sister-in-law, Miss Jane Dixon of Liverpool, he spent it on enlarging Holden Clough, near Bolton-by-Bowland, into a fine house. Tipping ran into financial trouble. Jane had no option but to foreclose on him and take over all his property. She left Liverpool in her own coach, followed by baggage wagons, and in Bowland found herself on roads that were glorified cart tracks. Her coach managed to negotiate the ford at Hell Syke, between Sawley and Bolton-by-Bowland, but the wagons were bogged down, leaving her without most of her personal belongings. Jane, her maid and the coachman stayed at a local inn until Holden Clough was in a good enough state to be occupied. An Irish boy who attended Stonyhurst College about 1815 spent a week of his holiday in travel. The lad, conspicuous in his uniform – blue swallow-tail coat, red waistcoat, buff-coloured knee breeches, blue or grey stockings – travelled by coach to Manchester, then by another coach to Liverpool. Here he boarded a cutter for the crossing of the Irish Sea.

130   *Stone-breakers on the road, from* The Costume of Yorkshire.

Packhorse trains, attended by jaggers, were for several centuries a familiar sight in Bowland, bringing in much needed supplies, such as salt, and taking away various products. So rough was the average Bowland road that a prudent mother using a horse-drawn trap would advise her children to sit on the bottom-boards in case they were tossed out. Summertime saw the patching of the 'waterbound' roads with a mixture of stones and soil, which were then sprinkled with water from a special horse-drawn cart. Local farmers on contract dumped stones at the roadside and old men promptly set about breaking them down to a suitably small size. The appearance of a steam-roller in a rural area caused a ripple of excitement. A farm lad would run a mile to see the roller at work and to coax the driver to give a few toots on the steam-whistle or blow jets of steam towards him.

Foot-sloggers included hawkers and gypsies, who sold pegs and inquired at the farms for fallen wool, rabbit or mole-skins. Odd-job men sought temporary work, such as scaling muck in the meadows. Tramps begged food and drink before kipping in a barn. Regular roadsters were tradesmen and salesmen, the emissaries of grocery firms situated in town, and butter-badgers. An itinerant tailor would stay at a farmhouse for a day or two, sitting in his customary cross-legged position near a window, which provided light. While he was making clothes, the farmer would provide his board and lodging.

No right of way existed through the township of Leagram-with-Little Bowland. Chains were kept across the roads near Chipping. The Trough road, a link between Lancaster and York, was the assize road used by judges. The retinue of the High Sheriff of Lancashire waited at the county boundary, listening for the sound of trumpets that foretold the arrival of the judge with his escort of lords and gentlemen of Yorkshire. Beside the old boundary stone, the judge was formally transferred from York to Lancaster. The mounted procession then continued on its way, through Wyresdale and Quernmore.

For some, the motor age began when Leonard King-Wilkinson, of Middlewood, toured the area in a De Dion steam car fired by paraffin. He explained to inquirers, 'If I gave it time to blow off steam at the bottom of a hill it would usually have the power to get to the top.' In the spring of 1928 a correspondent of the *Liverpool Post* found the Trough road, between Dunsop Bridge and Lancaster, was loose and gritty, gated here and there. The gates were 'usually open or well guide-posted'. He became heartily tired of 'the long grey line that seems to stretch to eternity up and down the hillsides'. The scenery was described as 'dreary', though 'perhaps later in the year, when the heather has taken on its green tips and the bracken its unfurling green standards, the outlook might be more acceptable.'

The Trough, on the Yorkshire side of the boundary, was to the newspaperman 'a curious zig-zag gash among queerly-cut hills'. Above Sykes farms it turns into a steep incline and 'climbs to the Lancashire moor'. Beyond the county boundary 'the road dips into a glen that might have escaped from Scotland. It has rose-stemmed firs, crystal-brown burns, larch, alder and hawthorn and the great expanse of moorland behind in which the shadows and mists can play and lurk.' Tramps preferred the Trough route to the main road north via Preston, which was overcrowded with 'cadger-bodies'. W.T. Palmer (1928) mentioned 'stone cairns which are said to have been piled on the bones of some vagrant found after a winter storm or dead with summer heat exhaustion'.

Allen Clarke, a chronicler of Lancashire life, described the 17 miles from Whitewell to Lancaster as 'lonesome'. For a dozen miles he and his companions saw 'only a couple of houses and only three or four folks, and one open carriage, with three persons in it; but never a cyclist, nor a motor car'. John L. Illingworth, a journalist of the 1930s, recalled bursting through the Trough on to the sudden spaciousness of Blaze Moor. 'There follows a swift descent from bleak upland to the sudden charm of the valley of the Wyre, here a crooning, chattering, bubble-blowing infant.' The change of landscape from open moor to the narrow valley known as Wyresdale was welcome to early road-users. The road kept close company with the beginnings of a river, the Marshaw Wyre, and stands of conifers gave the area a Scottish flavour.

Hereabouts lay the Forest of Wyresdale, where the old name of 'vaccary' was retained in a dozen townships that had their origins in the medieval settlements where cattle were bred and land farmed on behalf of the king. Since then the landscape had been 'improved' by successive landowners. In 1806 the gentleman called Fenton-Cawthorne reclaimed hundreds of acres from rush and ling, enclosing the land with drystone walls before sweetening it with lime burnt at a kiln at the road verge in the Trough. The trees he planted at the roadside were the forerunners of the giants of today. What Fenton-Cawthorne did for the upper valley, the Earls of Sefton did for the land lower down. They built a mansion and also farms and cottages. Gamekeepers managed the moors, which became highly productive of grouse.

Two roads from Slaidburn stormed the moorland heights beyond the upper Hodder. That connecting Slaidburn with Clapham reached its highest point at Bowland Knotts, a wind-strummed area of heather and outcropping gritstone, with a fair-weather view of the Three Peaks of Yorkshire. A parallel road to Bentham passed an erratic called the Great Stone of Fourstone (the other three stones sank or were chipped away by local farmers for sharpening tools).

Inns

Being on the York-Lancaster road, Slaidburn had trade for more than one inn.
The name *Hark to Bounty* (formerly *Dog Inn*) alluded to a hound whose melodious
calls were clearly heard above the chatter in the bar, the sound thrilling its owner,
a parson-cum-squire, the Rev. Henry Wigglesworth of Town Head, who kept a
pack of foxhounds. From about 1590 a building on the site was the setting for
the Halmote Court for the Forest of Bowland where minor disputes were settled.
A courtroom survived in a large upper room and was used for land tenures until
1920. Then, for over thirty years, it was locked up and virtually forgotten. When
it was reopened it became the venue for special functions such as wedding
receptions. The courtroom furnishings are still intact. For a time, George Rudd
looked after a branch of the Yorkshire Bank at the *Hark to Bounty* on specified
evenings, an amenity provided because Slaidburn was ten miles from the nearest
railway station or bank and the village might be cut off by snow for weeks on
end.

Slaidburn's other inn, the *Black Bull*, had an equally notable history. In the
churchwardens' accounts for 1764 is the item: 'Spent of the persons who brought
the slate from Ribchester at several times and other necessary meetings of the
Churchwardens as appears by the Bill
at *Black Bull* £1 5s. 5d.' Four years later,
when the inn was kept by the Winder
family, churchwardens' dinners and
expenses at the inn came to 5s. 2½d.
When the inn closed and was converted
into a youth hostel, the premises were
renamed King's House. The *De Lacy
Arms* at Whalley, formerly known as
Shoulder of Mutton, was built in the early
1860s on the site of the Manor House.
The *Three Fishes* at Mitton does not
relate to angling in the Ribble but to
the pattern on the abbey stones over
the door.

At *The Red Pump*, Bashall Eaves,
mine host combined inn-keeping with
farming on a small scale. If the press
gang was in the area, a likely lad might
be hidden under the hay in the barn.
Moorcock, beside the road crossing
Waddington Fell, was named after the
red grouse. In Chipping, where several
inns were to be found, an annual event

131 Hark to Bounty, *Slaidburn, an inn much
used by travellers.*

132 *The* Travellers Rest, *in the upper Hodder, was demolished by reservoir-builders.*

was a meeting of the all-male Henpeck Club which, having elected a Mayor, wheeled him round the village in a watercart. One year 30 worse-for-wear members were arrested.

Rail

When the railway connecting Blackburn with Clitheroe and West Yorkshire was opened it was described as one of the innumerable offspring of the 'railway mania' of 1845. In the autumn of that year no fewer than seven railway lines were proposed to pass through the town of Clitheroe in various directions. In 1847 an amalgamation of two proposals obtained parliamentary approval and led to the building of a line that was opened as far as Chatburn by 1850. Eventually it would connect with Hellifield. Stephen Clarke, reviewing the railway days in 1900, recalled the condemnation of the new system by 'those interested in the coaching and carrying business'. Old Peter Nowell, who worked at the *Boar's Head*, determined never to travel by rail. He kept his vow, even when, aged 70, he walked from Clitheroe to Barrowford to attend the funeral of a relative.

The railway transformed the appearance of the district, especially at Whalley, where the Calder Valley was spanned by a brick viaduct of many arches that by itself cost £40,000. George Clarke of Rishton, whose job was checking the quality and delivery of bricks, told Stephen Clarke that he had a horse at his command and rode and walked no less than 16 miles a day along the length. Thirteen brick-

133 *Impression of the Whalley railway viaduct, built from locally-made bricks.*

makers were employed at Whalley, the clay for the bricks being 'got' from the railway embankment. Bricks were made on either side of the line and were conveyed to where they were needed in wagons, then drawn up in wheelbarrows by horse-power, using ropes and pulleys. A barrow was let down by 'hooking the wheel'. The pier that was planned to stand in the bed of the Calder created special engineering problems. The river had a sandy bed and great baulks of timber and concrete were used to stabilise the brickwork.

134 *Newspaper drawing to mark the coming of the railway to Clitheroe, 1850.*

A writer in *The Preston Guardian* of June 1850 proudly asserted that 'the Blackburn and Clitheroe line will serve to connect several of the smokiest and most crowded marts of modern industry with some of the most venerable vestiges of antiquity and the most beautiful of Nature's retreats.' It would allow thousands of 'town-immured and toiling people' frequent opportunities of 'recruiting their health and of elevating their minds'. Soon after the opening of the line the stability of the Whalley viaduct was tested when two engines with trucks 'got off the metals at the Billington end. They were dragged ... over the arches, breaking the sleepers and chairs as they ploughed the ground.' When the line was in regular use, a favourite railway excursion was to the Preston Guild. In 1862 so many people used the trains that the coaches had to be supplemented by cattle wagons.

The Castle Museum collection at Clitheroe includes the ceremonial spade used by Lord Ribblesdale in 1874 when he cut the first sod at the start of the Chatburn to Hellifield extension of the Clitheroe Junction Railway. It had been intended to take the Lancashire and Yorkshire Railway from Chatburn to Hellifield through Bolton-by-Bowland, but Mr Wright, landowner, would not allow it to run through his park. It was not until 1878 that the line was extended to Chatburn, and in 1879 to Gisburn. The line to Hellifield was opened on 1 June 1880. After much bickering, Lord Ribblesdale allowed it to run through Gisburne Park providing a tunnel were made. The portals were stone-built, with castellations, and, as mentioned, it was his Lordship who cut the first sod.

Among the proposed but unrealised railway projects was a connection between Longridge and Hellifield, with stations at Whitewell, Slaidburn and Wigglesworth. An Act of Parliament was passed in 1917 but the capital subscribed fell short of requirements. From 1964 until 1994 the ten-mile stretch between Blackburn and Clitheroe was closed to passenger-carrying traffic. The Ribble Valley line had always been available for diversions and special trains but the re-establishment of a passenger service to Clitheroe came through the diligent efforts of local volunteers. The line from Clitheroe to Hellifield is used by freight traffic and steam-hauled special trains.

Buses

In 1912 engineers of the Fylde Water Board arrived by car at the hamlet of Stocks to put in hand work on a new reservoir. Theirs was the first motor vehicle to be seen in these parts. The first taxi in the district, a Model T Ford, commonly known as a 'Tin Lizzie', had an engine that was gravity fed, so the petrol tank had to be over half full when it was negotiating Dunnow Hill, near Slaidburn. A motor car created a sensation when it drew up outside *The Travellers' Rest* at Stocks Fold in 1919. A vicar who was departing from the parish hired a larger motor vehicle to move his possessions: 'When they started the engine, it struck fire. They soon put the fire out.'

In the early 1920s a bus of sorts ran between Bolton-by-Bowland and Clitheroe, the service initiated by Isaac Bleazard, who had previously had a taxi. Isaac's first bus was adapted from a lorry. It had a superstructure resembling a poultry cabin, with small side windows and a door at the back. The 'hut' was fitted with two fore and aft benches on which passengers sat facing each other. If they wanted to board or leave the bus, the driver had to leave his seat and carry a set of steps to the back. 'There were no official stopping places,' a local man recalls. 'One place was as good as another.'

The first motor bus to operate a regular service in Bowland was a Dennis, of 13.2 horse-power, belonging to Colin Walker of Slaidburn. He bought the engine and chassis in 1926 and fitted a saloon body. The brake, a plain rod, acted only on the back wheels. The tyres were pneumatic but the spare tyre was of solid rubber. Named the Bounty Motor Service, its route of eight-and-a-half miles involved a climb to 1,100 ft. The return fare from Slaidburn to Clitheroe was 3s. 6d. Petrol was purchased at Clitheroe in two-gallon cans. The gallant old bus ended its life on a scrap heap.

In the early 1920s the first motor 'bus raised the dust on the road 'back o' Pendle'. Owned by Adam Hargreaves, who had the mill at Barley, it was a 'convertible' used to transport the workpeople. The first real bus service was inaugurated by Edward Jones, who had a Ford 20-seater. For two decades, until it was taken over by Ribble in 1945, the Barley Bus Service operated between Nelson, Downham and Clitheroe, the fare from Barley to Nelson being 11d., passengers to Burnley paying an extra penny. The driver was known to do the shopping for homebound farmers' wives with young families. George Thomas Hartley of Newchurch, a carter, ran a service hauled by horses called Dolly and Polly. He took eggs and butter to markets in Burnley, returning to Newchurch with a load of coal. Butter cost between 1s. and 1s. 2d., eggs were a penny each and you might buy a hundred weight of coal for 4½d.

Bowland Transit, with fixed routes and a timetable, began operating in the spring of 2003. Modern buses have improved the mobility of Bowlanders who

135   *Car belonging to Fylde Water Board officials in the upper Hodder, c.1912.*

136   *A bus leaves Barley, c.1932.*

do not possess their own means of transport. The low floor buses are accessible for wheelchair and pushchair users and each vehicle has a cycle rack.

Telegraph

When, in 1890, Blackburn had completed its waterworks and appointed bailiffs to attend to the pipeline and other matters, it housed them at Dunsop and provided a Post Office telegraph so they could contact the Borough Engineer in Blackburn in an emergency. This was 'a matter of very grave importance when we remember that the nearest railway station is Clitheroe, 12½ miles away'. The telegraph went round by Slaidburn and became a convenience for several rich landowners who, in conjunction with Blackburn Corporation, guaranteed the Post Office business or subsidy of £128 a year. The Corporation's share was £16.

The house in which the bailiffs and their families lived – and where the telegraph was housed – became known as Bishop's House. The last tenant, a Roman Catholic ex-Bishop of Nottingham, retired to what he considered a secluded retreat and died there at the proverbial ripe old age.

Newspapers

The Clitheroe Advertiser and Times, which circulates widely throughout the area, and has a weekly sale of about 8,500 copies, resulted from the merger of two local newspapers in 1920. The first local newspaper dated from 1855 and had the cumbersome title of *Whewell's Family Newspaper and Clitheroe Monthly Advertiser.* The venture lasted two years. On 28 February 1885 John Cowgill launched *The Clitheroe Advertiser*, a free sheet published on Saturdays. *The Clitheroe Times*, founded by a printer, Richard Parkinson, was first published on 7 December 1888.

In 1963 the *Advertiser and Times* was sold by the Cowgill family to Provincial Newspapers Ltd., subsequently known as United Newspapers Ltd., who have a nationwide group of daily and weekly newspapers, with especially strong connections with Lancashire. This led to the first major mechanical change in the paper's history: it had been chiefly an eight-page paper printed on a flat-bed press; four pages were run off during the day on Thursday, followed by the second four on Thursday night and early Friday morning. Its new owners transferred the printing to Blackburn and the paper was run off on a rotary press in about an hour. Larger papers, with more pictures, now became the norm.

In 1972 the paper became part of the *Burnley Express* and a member of the North East Lancashire Press Group that includes the *Nelson Leader* and *Colne Times* series. In the summer of 1974 photo-setting and computerisation were introduced.

Twelve

WATER FOR THE TOWNS

Blackburn

Long before Liverpool and Manchester were drawing water supplies from North Wales and Lakeland respectively, Blackburn drew water from the Brennand Valley and Whitendale, in remoter Bowland. J.G. Shaw, who researched the undertaking, wrote in 1891: 'Our pipes come over Kemple End, 565 ft above the level of the sea, and down through the Ribble Valley where the elevation is only 102 ft.' The length of the main was over 20 miles. The Falls of Brennand were 'the furthest interesting point of our gathering ground'. The cascade, situated half a mile above a conduit, 'is in such an out-of-the-way place in the Forest of Bowland … that it is very rarely seen, even by gentlemen who visit the waterworks'. This was considered to be the prettiest area; 'next to it we should place the two Costy Cloughs [in Whitendale] which are more easily accessible.'

137 *Wally Blackwell and the steam locomotive* Fylde *during the construction of Stocks Reservoir.*

Compensation water for the river Dunsop was measured 'with the greatest delicacy and accuracy' at the Clock House, the elevation of which was about 1,300 ft. Eighty men employed in the Brennand Valley lead mines had occupied a nearby block of four cottages in the 1860s. The proposal to build a compensation reservoir was shelved when a compromise was reached with the riparian owners all the way down the Dunsop and Hodder to the junction with the Ribble at Mitton. Having

138   *Remains of the mineral line connecting Jumbles Quarry with the dam at Stocks.*

purchased their rights under an Act of 1877, the Corporation abandoned the reservoir project and reduced the flow of compensation water. The Brennand became a trickle after the Corporation 'turned as much as they want of it into the mouth of our immense cast-iron pipes, 30 inches in diameter, at a point higher up the valley'.

At the delightfully named Costy Clough, in Whitendale, stood a mission room for the navvies engaged in the waterworks. One Victorian visitor found, in the largest of the now ruinous huts, a rude pulpit and forms. Two bailiffs capable of effecting repairs in an emergency lived at Dunsop Houses. Their 'beat' extended from the head of the waterworks to the Hodder at Sandalholme, which was nearly half way to Blackburn. The men walked round the works daily, measuring and collecting the rainfall, attending to the purity of the town's supply and the regularity of the compensation water. They had also to 'make themselves generally useful'. An iron bridge near Thorneyholme, on the Hodder, served the double purpose of carrying the pipes and a footpath across the water. The bridge was given an elegant appearance in deference to a branch of the Towneley family, with whom the Corporation had chiefly to deal when buying land and water rights, who lived at a local mansion.

The town (now city) of Preston impounded the Langden, a tributary of the Hodder.

139 *The Hodder near Cross o' Greet, main feeder of Stocks Reservoir.*

140 *Hindley Head, Dalehead, on the catchment of Stocks Reservoir.*

141   *Remains of the hospital used during the construction of Stocks Reservoir.*

Pendle

East Lancashire towns took advantage of the high rainfall by constructing reservoirs on either side of the village of Barley. Upper and Lower Black Moss reservoirs lie to the north of the village. Nelson Corporation built two reservoirs in the upper reach of Ogden Clough, the filter being made in part from what had been a 200-loom cotton mill that was seriously damaged by flooding in 1880.

Stocks Reservoir

An especially dry and hot summer forcibly reminded the Fylde Water Board of the need to enlarge the area of supply. An Act of 1912 enabled the Board to acquire compulsorily 9,500 acres of the shallow basin of the upper Hodder. The value of each farm was calculated according to the rent paid for the previous 20 years so purchase was achieved at the bargain price of £150,000 or £15 an acre. Nature had been good to reservoir-builders. Long-melted glaciers had smeared the sides of the valley with impervious clay and Harry Cottam (resident engineer) found suitable rock at what became known as Jumbles Quarry when, during a picnic with his wife and two small sons, he investigated a likely area. He returned to the family with the news that he had an ample source of gritstone capable of being worked by masons but tough enough for use on the dam.

The flooding of 244 acres of the best pastureland in the valley caused the hamlet of Stocks and several farms to be lost. Additionally, 26 farms and cottages in the catchment area were abandoned. The Board's negotiations were with absentee landlords, leaving the tenantry in ignorance of their intentions. The paperwork was carried out before the First World War, and when the first machines moved in some of the farmers believed they were preparing the ground for an Army camp. The war prevented an early start on the reservoir. Around 1916, visiting officials and engineers were accommodated in what had been the *Travellers' Rest* and the smithy was used as a workshop.

Four reservoirs had been projected but a second, more detailed, geological survey indicated that it was safe to raise the high water level to a capacity equal to all four. Not until 1920 did work begin in earnest. In 1923, supplies for the reservoir were being transported from railway sidings at Long Preston to Tosside on wagons drawn by traction engines. From here the material was borne to the site of the dam. A 3ft. gauge railway was built at a cost of £10,000.

Historic Grange Hall and its attendant copse were cleared away as a matter of urgency. The reservoir-builders wanted to use gravel from the bed on which they stood. Mrs Cowking, the last tenant of Grange, was a widow with five children. As she prepared to leave for a new home in a horse-drawn cart, two Water Board officials noticed she had piled some old straw in the bottom. In due course, a letter from head office at Blackpool demanded to know why she was taking the straw and explained how much she might be fined for such a crime.

142 *Dalehead church, demolished and replaced by a smaller building.*

143 *The school at Dalehead, 1913.*

Mrs Cowking had the last word: the letter arrived at the time of Dalehead Sports, which the two officials had decided to visit; mother approached them in front of a crowd and gave them a piece of her mind. They had no option but to apologise.

Work began with the excavation of a trench down to bedrock, the sides being shored-up by heavy timber. Four electric cranes lifted excavated soil and rock, the material being tipped into railway wagons and taken away. The trench was then filled with puddled clay to ground level and, as work proceeded, to the very top of the dam. At its peak, the labour force reached just over 500 men. Most of them were housed in Hollins, a shanty village. Navvies came and went. A large building was available for social purposes and also served as a cinema, an irresistible, twice-a-week attraction featuring epics such as *Rin Tin Tin*, a novelty for workmen and people from the farms. Each navvy was rationed to two pints of beer, to be imbibed at lunch-time. Drink accounted for much of the wage of £2 5s. a week. Hard liquor was banned but – said a despairing official – the men made up for it by drinking enough beer and stout to sink a battleship. A man developed a thirst by cooking himself plenty of kippers. The evils of drink and gambling were challenged by the Church and by emissaries of the Church Army.

The Bishop of Bradford consecrated the new graveyard in November 1926, and the transfer of bodies from the former graveyard took place in the following

144 *Worthies of Dalehead, 1931. The vicar, the Rev. C. Slater, and H. P. Killick, headmaster, are standing.*

145 *The Boardroom, Stocks Reservoir, was largely constructed from stone taken from demolished farmsteads.*

146 *A stone for the pumping station constructed by Nelson Waterworks near Barley in 1912.*

147 *A metal indicator relating to Blackburn Waterworks.*

year. The remains were reverently placed in large pine coffins and moved to their new quarters at dead of night, using a horse and flat cart. One who saw the process said, 'They had a storm lantern on the cart so they could see where they were going. It did look weird.' Remarkably, the only death occurred when Brian, one of the twin sons of the resident engineer, was gravely injured. Unbeknown to his father, he had left the railcar on which he was being given a ride when the car stopped briefly so father could discuss a matter with a workman. Brian was run over when father resumed the journey, not knowing his son was not on board. He died from his injuries. He was to have occupied the first new grave to be dug at Dalehead but his grieving mother, not wanting such a lonely situation for

148 *The water pipeline over the Hodder was constructed by Blackburn Waterworks.*

him, persuaded Mr King-Wilkinson to allow the burial to take place in part of his family's plot at Slaidburn.

On 5 July 1932 the valve was opened on Stocks Reservoir. The amount of compensation water needed to satisfy the Hodder's riparian owners was originally six-and-a-half million gallons a day. Harry Cottam was fond of saying that enough water was sent down the river to keep the fish wet. No fish pass was allowed for and migratory species like salmon and sea trout had their range restricted. Above the dam, the rotting of expanses of vegetation for a time sustained an increased amount of insect life on which the brown trout throve. With relatively few anglers – inquirers were told no fish remained – the Board members and their friends enjoyed excellent sport.

149 *Falls of Brennand, a feeder for Blackburn Waterworks.*

Thirteen

An Update

Lord Harry Scott, who became Lord Montagu of Beaulieu, eventually held the Castle and Honour of Clitheroe. His son administered the Clitheroe estates through the Clitheroe Estate Company Limited. The Castle and the Honour were separated in 1919. A public subscription list was opened to buy the Castle and grounds extending to 17 acres as the town's war memorial. The Honour remained in the ownership of the Clitheroe Estate Company until 1945. The Hon. Ralph Assheton of Downham Hall then bought it. When he was created a Baron, in 1955, he assumed the title of Lord Clitheroe of Downham.

The 16th-century manor house set in the midst of the ruins of the Cistercian abbey at Whalley was restored in the 19th century and is now a retreat and conference house under the auspices of Blackburn diocese. The imposing 17th-century *Ribblesdale Arms Hotel* at Gisburn – a Grade II listed building – with its outbuildings has been splendidly conserved and adapted as residential accommodation. Stephen Park, which is reached along a Forest Enterprises track in the new Forest of Gisburn, provides a heartening instance of the re-use of an old farmstead as a leisure and training complex. Parts of the building are over three centuries old. Many of the ceilings have oak beams. This group of buildings, of Grade II classification, is run by Knowsley Council for Voluntary Service, on Merseyside. Within the stout walls is first-class accommodation for visitors. A purpose-built conference room can accommodate up to 50 people. The ICT Barn next to the main building has state-of-the-art computer and IT facilities and a second conference suite.

Restoration plans at the vast limestone quarry in the Ribble Valley have been designed to encourage large new areas of species-rich calcareous grassland to develop over time. Using a specially formulated 'nurse crop' of fine grasses, together with local seed and turves, large new areas of flower-rich meadow will develop. Almost all of this type of flower and insect-rich grassland had been lost through changes in farming practices over the last century. At the Lanehead quarry, quarrymen are helping to build a database of flora and fauna. Nesting birds include peregrine falcon, oystercatcher and little ringed plover. The floral range includes the bee orchid.

Now that tourism is a major industry in rural areas, it is amusing to ponder on conditions 70 years ago, when one motorist on the 30 miles of 'soft' road between Lancaster and Bashall Eaves found he had to open and shut several gates. Intruders on the moors were not welcome. Today, moorland safaris are organised by the RSPB, English Nature and United Utilities – who acquired the water undertaking – in search of Bowland's special birds. The walk leaders explain how the moors are managed for birds, for farming and for the quality of the water that comes through the tap.

Tourism has become a major source of income. Signs proliferate, many having the chocolate-hue indicating features of special interest. There are tucked-away features like the nursery at Holden Clough, near Bolton-by-Bowland, which years ago was regularly visited by Reginald Farrer, 'father' of rock gardening, who was once so moved by a shrub he prostrated himself before it. At Pendleton an inn doubles as a post office. The Sabden handloom weavers of old were said to weave parkin, using oatmeal as the warp and treacle as the weft. Visitors to All Hallows' Church at Mitton, the story of which spans over seven centuries, may use a new staircase to the Tower Room and the gallery. There is a chair lift.

Those who drive to Stonyhurst in bright weather will not forget the scene on the road leading from Hurst Green. Having left woodland shade and made a 90-degree bend, they see half a mile of unfenced road crossing verdant grassland to where two huge ponds mirror the palatial buildings, towers and cupolas of the Jesuit college – a building listed as Grade I. Stonyhurst has undergone a technological revolution. From the start of the new academic year in September 2003, pupils had free, filtered access to the Internet from all round the college. Despite its rural location, the College has kept up with the broadband revolution. A dish has been concealed on the roof of the building making high-speed Internet access possible from a radio transmission station at Wiswell.

Among the fascinating objects on show within the College is the desk bearing the name A.C. Doyle, Arthur Ignatius Conan Doyle, a not very distinguished pupil here between 1868 and 1875. He was to achieve a lasting reputation as the creator of Sherlock Holmes, and Dr Watson. The Yew Alley, in which the fictional Sir Henry Baskerville had a fatal heart attack while running from a phantom hound, is based on the Dark Walk in the Stonyhurst garden.

Stonyhurst remembers with pride its association with a master storyteller of modern times. John Ronald Reuel Tolkien (1892-1973), Reader in English Language at the University of Leeds and subsequently Oxford Professor of Anglo-Saxon and later of English Language and Literature, worked on his epic *The Lord of the Rings* trilogy for a dozen years. A favoured place for reflection and writing was a classroom in the upper gallery of Stonyhurst, with which his sons John and Michael were associated. During the Second World War, John, who had been studying for the priesthood at the English College in Rome, was evacuated to the Jesuit seminary at St Mary's Hall (now the preparatory school for Stonyhurst College). Michael taught classics at the College and at St Mary's Hall in the late 1960s and 1970s. A Tolkien Trail has been devised, with an explanatory leaflet.

Summer events, when visitors mingle with local folk, include the agricultural shows at Chipping, Longridge and in the Hodder Valley. A writer in the *Clitheroe Advertiser* noted, 'Bands play, the tea is strong and hot. Cakes are scrumptious.' The shaggy cattle of Old Bowland have been supplanted by the Longhorn, which in turn gave way to the Shorthorn, which in its turn was ousted by the Friesian from the Low Countries. The beef breeds that endure are Angus and Galloway cattle, plus some handsome and profitable continental strains with names that, at first, were not easy to pronounce – Charolais, Limousin, Belgian Blue, Simmental and Blonde d'Aquitaine. A recent change in the pattern of hill farming is allowing history to repeat itself, however, with the introduction of beef produced in an organic way that abhors pesticides, herbicides, genetically modified seed and the antibiotics that had been used routinely.

At Meldingscales, a 165-acre holding rented from Ingleborough Estate, a fall in the price received for milk, from 28p. to 16p. a litre, resulted in the farmer, David Burns, working at a loss. He decided the dairy cows should be put to a beef bull, but beef production being not much better than milk financially, he opted for organic methods. Working to the standards of the Soil Association, he gives his cattle abundant space in clover-rich pastures. In winter the stock is kept in roomy straw-yards. The old dairy has been converted into a refrigerated store for meat that is sold directly to customers, mainly at the farm gate, in 10kg. boxes.

Meanwhile, one of the 40 herds of White Park cattle featuring in the herd book and associated historically with Whalley and Gisburn, is well established near Chipping, in Bowland. There is disagreement about the origin of what is undeniably an ancient breed. Some have claimed it is descended in direct line from the Aurochs of the Wildwood. Others date its appearance in England from Roman times. Blood-protein analysis indicates that the breed is far removed from all our other cattle – so different, indeed, that commercial breeders regard them as a source of hybrid vigour in crossing programmes. Calves by White Park bulls, whose lineage goes back for over a millennium, have outperformed those sired by Herefords, Welsh Blacks and Limousins.

A group of Bowland farmers has established a co-operative to promote local products under the title Bowland Forest Foods. Initially, meats included lamb, beef, pork and free-range chicken. The cheese-making industry has been transformed during the last two decades, with old recipes being revived and new recipes created. Chipping is at the heart of the Lancashire cheese country. Timothy Procter founded the Wolfen Mill Dairy Company in 1934 to help farmers who were producing unpasteurised cheese in their homes. A redundant barn on the Leagram Estate was granted planning permission for conversion to a dairy which uses organic milk to produce, mainly, cheese of the Lancashire variety.

150 *The Park at Gisburn owned by the Lords Ribblesdale. Their mansion is now a private hospital.*

The Pendle Witch Trail, extending over 45 miles, follows a route from Pendleside villages through the Trough of Bowland to Lancaster. Gisburn Forest, in the catchment of Stocks Reservoir, now has cycleways as well as well-marked footpaths. A circular walk begins and ends at Gisburn. The Lancashire Cycleway consists of a north and south circular route that meet at Whalley. Minor roads are used as much as possible. Some off-road routes are designed for the especial use of mountain bikes. Off-road cycling is catered for on the Lune Millennium Cycleway. Pendle Hill, noted for its updraughts, is used by paragliders, and the Pendle Soaring Club has over 200 active members, some of whom achieve altitudes in excess of 4,000ft. and flights of over 100 km. A clear-weather view from a glider soaring above Pendle or above another field at Beacon Hill takes in both west and east coasts, as well as the mountains in Wales, Lakeland and Scotland.

Conifer plantations smother what had been bare ridges and hills, especially in the east. More enlightened planting schemes and the introduction of some deciduous species are changing the monotonous appearance. A commercial forestry enterprise originated by the Forestry Commission takes in 25 scattered woods in the Hodder Valley, a large contiguous area north-east of Stocks Reservoir and a portion of Grindleton Fell. Scots pine give a British flavour to areas dominated by introductions – sitka spruce and lodgepole pine from North

America, Japanese larch and Norwegian spruce. Thinning of the plantations at Stocks started in 1972.

Free-ranging Japanese sika and roe deer have replaced the red and fallow deer of the old Forest days. In the AONB are 456 wildlife sites – known in Lancashire as Biological Heritage Sites – covering about ten per cent of the area. Stocks Reservoir, owned by United Utilities, is a prime bird-watching site. Anglers, operating from boats, also use it. Beacon Fell Country Park, at the southern edge of the Bowland Fells, is a tract of rough moorland and woodland covering 185 acres. Established in 1969, it was one of the first Country Parks to be recognised by the Countryside Agency. The Fell rises in grand isolation to an elevation of 873ft/266m. Early Viking settlers used the area as a *saeter*, livestock taking advantage of the summer flush of grass. Today the woodland is being made more varied. Coniferous tracts planted when Beacon Fell was a gathering ground for a water authority are enhanced by native trees such as rowan, birch, alder and oak. Siskin and crossbill are among the birds recorded in the woodland. The slopes of Spade Meadow are used for sledging and ski-ing in winter.

Pendle has provided a backdrop for a film and television series. *Whistle Down the Wind*, starring Hayley Mills and Alan Bates, was a whimsical drama concerning three children who believe that a fugitive killer hiding out at a Lancashire farm is Jesus Christ. A television series, *Born and Bred*, first transmitted in 2002, was memorable for its Downham setting, Pendle Hill providing an imposing backdrop. The Hill now has a Commoners' and Graziers' Association. Their aim – the better management of the Hill – has the support of other user groups.

The special character of Bowland is being recognised at international level. In 2001 the Lancashire County Council and English Heritage began a three-year project, part of a European initiative relating to historic landscape. It was to include 12 projects from ten countries. The English project is focusing on the Forest of Bowland and the Lune Valley, the history of this culturally distinctive area having been largely overlooked in the past. The project – and this book – are timely since this area, like many another, is under increasing pressure for change.

BIBLIOGRAPHY

Ackerley, Frederick George, *History of Mitton* (1947)

Ainsworth, Harrison, *The Lancashire Witches* (1848)

Bennett, Walter, *The Pendle Witches* (1957)

Borough of Pendle, *The Pendle Way* (1986)

Brazendale, David, *Lancashire's Historic Halls* (1994)

Brigg, Mary, *The Early History of the Forest of Pendle* (1989)

Clarke, Stephen, *Clitheroe in its Railway Days* (1900)

Collins, Herbert C., *The Roof of Lancashire* (1950)

Crainer, Stuart, *A History of Chipping* (1986)

Dixon, John, *Historic Walks in the Ribble Valley* (1987)

Dobson, William, *Rambles by the Ribble* (1864)

Fell, Jimmy, *Window on Whalley* (1979)

Fletcher, J.S., *A Picturesque History of Yorkshire, vol 3* (1901)

Greenwood, M. and Bolton, C., *Bolland Forest and the Hodder Valley* (1955, 2000)

Houghton, A.T.R., *The Ribble Salmon Fisheries* (1952)

Johnson, Thos, *A Pictorial Handbook to the Valley of the Ribble* (1884)

Leigh, Val and Podmore, Brian, *Outstanding Churches in Craven* (1985)

Lofthouse, Jessica, *Three Rivers* (1946); *Round about Clitheroe* (1961); *Lancashire Countrygoer* (1962); *North-Country Folk Lore* (1976)

Lord, A.R., *Wolves, Chipping Local History Society journal* (1991)

Milne-Redhead, Richard, *Recollections of a Country Gentleman* (1977)

Mitchell, W.R., *Lancashire Witch Country* (1966); *The Lost Village of Stocks-in-Bowland* (1992); *Stocks Re-visited* (1993); *The Walker's Guide to Bowland and Pendle* (1993); *Life and Traditions of the Ribble Valley* (1994)

Neill, Robert, *Mist over Pendle*, a novel (1951)

Peel, Edgar and Southern, Pat, *The Trials of the Lancashire Witches* (1969)

Potts, Thomas, *The Wonderful Discovery of Witches in the County of Lancashire* (1613)

Preston Guardian, The, *Ribble Valley Railway* (22 June 1850)

Rackham, Oliver, *The History of the Countryside* (1986)

Raistrick, Arthur, *Lead Mining in the Mid-Pennines* (1973)

Sellers, Gladys, *The Ribble Way* (1985);*Walking in the Forest of Bowland* (1994)

Shaw, J.G., *Notes on Blackburn Waterworks* (1891)

Shepley, Alan, *Lancashire Rambles* (1992)

Smith, Tom C., *History of the Parish of Chipping* (1894)

Sowden, M.A. and Pickles, P.F., *The Manufacture of Cement at Ribblesdale* (1995)

Spiby, Cyril, *Walking in Bowland and Pendle* (1984)

Stonyhurst College, *Stonyhurst Handbook* (1947); *Leaflet – In the Steps of J.R.R. Tolkien* (2003)

Whitaker, T.D., *History of Whalley* (1801); *History and Antiquities of Craven* (1805)

Winder, John William, *Pudseys and Parsons* (1972)

INDEX

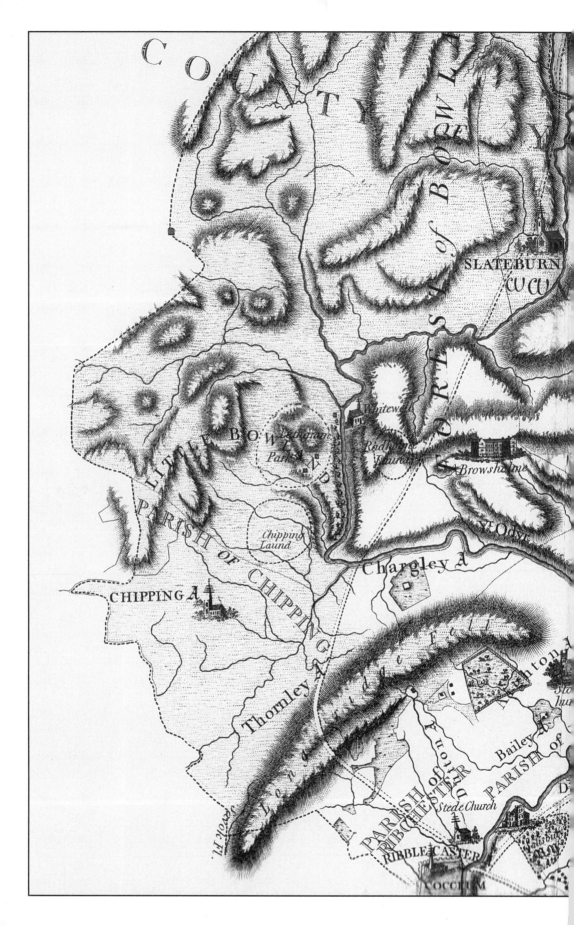

COUNTY

FOREST of BOWLAND

SLATEBURN

CU CU

Whitewell

Radholme Laund

Browsholme

St. Olive

LITTLE BOWLAND

Lathgnam Park

PARISH of CHIPPING

Chipping Laund

Chargley A

CHIPPING A

Thornley

Loui

Leagram hill

Knighton

Sto hur

Bailey

PARISH of

PARISH of RIBCHESTER

Stede Church

D

Dutton

Frou

RIBBLE CASTER

Salisbury

COCCIUM